Among Friends
Stories from the Journey

by
Father Jim Sichko
with Chas Allen and Jonathan Ryan

Among Friends

eISBN: 978-1-62467-227-9
Print ISBN: 978-1-62467-228-6

Published by Premier Digital Publishing
www.premierdigitalpublishing.com
Follow us on Twitter @PDigitalPub
Follow us on Facebook: Premier Digital Publishing

Dedication

This book is dedicated to my mother,
Marie C. Sichko, and to those I am called to serve.

Marie C. Sichko

A portion of the proceeds from all sales of this book will go toward the John Besh Foundation and the Diocese of Lexington Seminary Fund.

Foreword

It has been several years ago now that I received a rather peculiar donation to our foundation along with a note left at the hostess stand at my restaurant, *August*, familiarly written by a Father Jim, whom I didn't recall ever having met. The note, more or less a modern-day epistle, explained how he had been on a mission trip to my home town and had subsequently profited from his preaching and wanted to donate it to a great cause in the New Orleans area, where he had attended our Notre Dame Seminary. The epistle reminded me that we are all called to be stewards of our gifts. What struck me as impressive was that Father Jim, a priest who constantly gives of his time, energy, and talents, did, in fact, feel obliged to share his meager wages among the community that he was evangelizing.

Admittedly poor with names, I began exploring my mental Rolodex of priestly friends, and, for the life of me, I couldn't remember ever meeting a Father Jim. Without a business card or much of any contact information other than what was on the Richmond, Kentucky, bank check, I had no clue as to who this generous fellow was. Before I had the chance to draft a proper thank-you, I spoke with my mother, Imelda, as I do every morning. She began recalling uplifting and entertaining stories of this Father Jim, a former thespian and opera singer, whom she had heard at a Lenten workshop given by my very own St. Luke the Evangelist Parish. She went on to tell me that, as this week-long retreat progressed, Father Jim would entertain the congregation with recounting each and every course of food he had dined on at several of our restaurants — along with the interactions between him and my staff — while in town. Using these seemingly everyday occurrences, he conveyed the teachings and lessons of Christ that are alive and ever-present in all of our lives. Though Imelda and I visit every day, and spirituality is often a favored topic, I've never heard Mother so enthused — or, for that matter, entertained — by a guest speaker at church.

As it turns out, Father Jim and I would eventually meet and become great friends, not through the obvious church connection but, rather, through food. By breaking bread at both my family table and his, I have been blessed to share a sacred bond with him, his family, and his adoptive family in Kentucky. This dynamic and entertaining teacher, even while at a table among friends, has a way not only of challenging us to be the Christians that we are called to be but also of comforting us with the love of God — knowing that, although none of us are perfect, we are loved by the ever-so-merciful Father. I am fortunate to know this man who, through the everyday comedy of his life, brings us closer to the spiritual realities of every story in our lives and the way we are called to address them.

John Besh
Celebrity Chef and Restaurateur

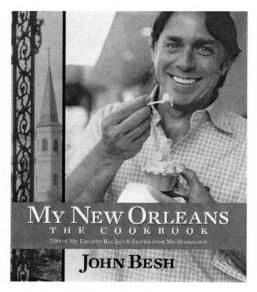

Chef John Besh

A Note from Chas Allen

It has been an honor and a privilege to have the opportunity to work on the compilation of this book. Not only was it an incredible and uplifting project to be a part of, but, over the course of the past six months, I have come to know Father Jim not only as a priest and motivational speaker, but also as a friend.

When he taught at the Catholic high school I attended, I was always impressed by his teaching methods. I wasn't always thrilled with them — especially when he would reprimand me with detention for talking during class. Nonetheless, I always respected his ability to teach and get results.

I have come to know Father Jim in a way that I feel most do not. I've had the privilege to be his co-author, personal trainer, and life-coach over the past six months. Father Jim has been an inspiration to me. He is one of the most selfless individuals I have ever encountered. He will go to the ends of the earth if it will help someone else — or even just bring the slightest smile to that person's face.

His traveling and his speaking are reflections of his deep-seated desire to benefit others, and he does. I've seen, on many occasions, the effect that he is able to have on people's lives. With care, concern, his entertaining personality, his quick wit, or any of the gifts he is blessed with, he is able to have a positive impact on all who happen to be fortunate enough to encounter him. I have seen it not only on a wide scale but also on a personal level.

I am sincerely thankful for the opportunity to work with Fr. Jim, but, most of all, for the opportunity to come to know him as a person and friend. He believed in me, when doing so wasn't easy. He was willing to get to know me and accept me for who I am today, and not for who I was years past. He is always teaching, always leading by example, which is reminiscent of none other than the supreme example, Jesus Christ. It is with great humbleness and gratitude that I thank him for inviting me to share this journey with him. I also thank each of you who happen to be reading these words for joining us on the journey as well. I hope it has been as much a joy and positive influence on your lives as it has been on mine.

Chas Allen

A Note from Jonathan Ryan

On a beautiful summer night, I sat drinking strong coffee and watching Father Jim in his natural habitat, among friends. He sat with a group of people he calls his "second family." Father, Ben and Regina Invergo, their kids, extended family from Austria, and I ate, laughed, joked and teased each other over an amazing meal.

I looked around the horse farm, watching the smiling faces, with Father Jim in the midst of it all, and I remember thinking, "This is what heaven will be like."

In our broken world, we live with a lot of sadness, pain and sorrow. My own life is a story of all three, as I journeyed from the Catholic Church, into Protestant ordination, and now find myself back where I started: a "sign of the cross," Jesus-eating, kneeling, committed Catholic.

Father Jim came into my life right in the midst of that transition as he asked me to help with his book. As a paranormal/horror writer, my usual job is to make up terrifying monsters, spooky ghosts, and scary people to read about on a blustery night when the veil between worlds is thin. I didn't know how I would do helping with a creative non-fiction book.

When I got Father Jim's manuscript, I couldn't help but be drawn in by his stories. They made me laugh. They made me cry. They made me want to help draw out this God-gifted storyteller into the printed word. I wanted to help Father Jim put the final touches on his manuscript.

So after weeks of editing, rewriting and a visit to Kentucky horse country, we finished the book.

Read it in the light of day. Read it in the darkest of nights. Father Jim's stories will help you open the door to heaven, and the Holy Spirit will walk you through it.

Jonathan Ryan
Written on the feast day of St. Martha

The Beginning...

Ancient Jewish Rabbis put together books called "Midrash." These books consisted of stories, reflections, and speculations on the Hebrew Bible (or Old Testament for Christians). The teachers wanted people to read these stories and reflect on them to find deeper meaning in God's word.

This book is my Midrash. In addition to being a priest for fifteen years, I've traveled all over the world. I've preached to many different cultures and people. I've learned to say prayers in different languages. Although I can't claim the wisdom of the ancient Jewish sages, I've learned a lot through my own mistakes and crazy experiences.

Along the way, I've met a lot of people (especially Highway State Troopers), and listened to their stories. I've included their tales, my experiences, and God's word in my talks. People seem to love them and I love seeing their reactions. I love moving people to tears, laughter, and watching them embrace a deep sense of joy found in God. Somehow, He uses my life to transform people and help them find His Good News in the person of Jesus Christ.

Really, what more could I want?

For many years, people kept telling me I needed to write a book and put all my stories in one place. Finally, I broke down, opened my computer, and hammered it out. I discovered a newfound admiration for those who can turn a phrase on the printed page. As I sat at my desk, sweating, drinking vast amounts of water and looking at a dictionary, I realized God didn't call me to be a writer. I'm a preacher, and I admire people who can string words together and make sense.

Still, as you hold this book in your hand – via old-fashioned print or a new-world e-reader or tablet – you know I made it through alive.

As I learned in every part of life and ministry, no goal is ever accomplished alone. This book, *Among Friends*, is a product of hard work with my own personal scribes, Chas Allen and Jonathan Ryan, both authors and fantastic writers in their own right.

Believe it or not, I taught Chas in ninth grade at a Catholic high school. Years later, our paths crossed again when Chas got involved in an art heist. One of the largest art thefts in history, Chas found himself on international news outlets, and I recognized him as a former student.

Although I prayed for him on a daily basis, I couldn't visit him during his six-year sentence in federal prison. He told me later about the isolation, embarrassment, and humiliation. Still, he drew closer to Christ through the experience and repented of his sins.

After Chas paid his debt to society, our paths crossed once again, and we began communicating. His knowledge, rooted in the journey of his faith, and gift for the written word impressed me on all levels. A published author himself, we started talking about my book. He offered to help me in writing up my little Midrash for people to take home after one of my talks.

I met Jonathan through a parishioner's daughter who is now my literary agent. He just completed a horror mystery novel that will be in bookstores October 2013. His natural ability to spin a yarn on the page made him a natural choice to help me hone my stories. Just know, unlike his book, mine won't keep you peeping around the corners and sleeping with the lights on.

And, so, the journey began.

Allow me to give you a word of advice for when you read this book at bedtime or in the morning at the coffee house. Don't read it straight through like a novel. You'll notice that I jump around, tell stories and give personal reflections. I did that on purpose. I want you to enjoy the book by reflecting on it, talking about it, and letting it transform you.

You might even disagree with much of it, and that's great. Just tell everyone why.

Like the Midrash of the ancient Jewish scholars, I hope it prompts you to talk about God's word, His love and the mystery of His presence. Many of the stories are just as they happened. Many are imaginative retellings of real events. Some are just plain made up to make a larger point.

And what is that point?

As a priest in Christ's church, I hope it draws you closer to the One who rules our lives, made the world and died for our sins.

So, let's reason, laugh, cry, and walk together through this Midrash. Amen? Amen.

Booted

"Jim, I would like to talk to you at the retreat center right away."

I swallowed hard as I held the phone. When the priest in charge of your ordination studies says those words, it tends to put you on edge. The grim and serious tone in his voice didn't help matters.

"Um, can I ask what this is about, Father?"

"Just please come out to the retreat center, Jim."

"I've just packed my car and am ready to go back to New Orleans—"

"To continue your studies after Christmas break, yes, I know. Right now, please."

With a terse good-bye, he hung up.

As I drove to the retreat center, a ton of bad thoughts ran through my mind. I thought through every scenario, but nothing made sense.

What could possibly be wrong? My evaluations from Notre Dame Seminary in New Orleans were excellent from all my professors and teachers. No one filed a complaint against me, or seemed to object to me pursuing the priesthood. Maybe, I thought, someone committed a paperwork snafu after all the chaos in the diocese at the moment. The bishop, my personal mentor, had passed away a few months before following a battle with brain cancer. As expected, it left things in a bit of a mess with no replacement named. I knew everyone was playing catch-up, and maybe Father wanted to see me to tie some loose ends.

Still, I couldn't shake the feeling that something wasn't right. As I drove into the parking lot, I took a few deep breaths.

Come on, Jim, get a grip. It's probably nothing.

I walked into Father's office and he didn't smile.

A bad sign.

"Jim, I'm going to make this short. You're no longer allowed to continue studying. You're being dismissed from your studies."

I felt as if he had punched me in the face. In some ways, I wish he had.

"Why? I don't understand . . . I mean–"

"There is no room for discussion, Jim. I suggest you go back home and find something else to do with your life."

I didn't say anything and got up to leave. As I sat in my car for a moment, tears welled up in my eyes and my stomach churned. Everything I'd worked for the past few years was gone. I felt betrayed by the church I loved. I gave my life for her and she slapped me in the face.

This can't be happening. It just can't be happening.

I started to drive home.

Everything, I'd given up everything. Ever since I was a boy, I wanted to be a priest. Now, it was all over, done.

Twenty years later, the pain of that experience still feels a bit raw. Many people ask me about that feeling of rejection. They want to know how it felt to be thrown out with no explanation.

From the look on their faces, I can tell they don't understand why I didn't just give up and find a different career.

The unspoken questions are: Why didn't you just go and do something else? Being a priest is hard, right? Why didn't you just leave it alone?

It's true: being a priest is hard, and maybe I'm just a bit crazy. In fact, I am crazy, but that's not why I'm a priest. I mean, it's not exactly a normal thing to want to be a priest. God's call is a huge part of it, and it doesn't come to many people.

This priestly call is about giving up what many people consider important or what brings joy. Priests give up the idea of offspring of their own. They give up marrying a woman to walk through life with them. To many people in our culture, this makes no sense at all.

I've often wracked my brain for ways to explain it to others. So, I came up with this explanation: those of us called to the priesthood exchange some joys for others. The joys we get in return are to serve God, His people, and lead them to change the world through His Grace. And, the past fifteen years as a priest have given me a vast amount of joy.

So, how did I get that call?

Let me tell you a story about that...

Even though I was born in Pittsburgh, I grew up in Orange, a small town in Southeast Texas. I was raised in a Slovak/Italian Catholic family. The church acted as our community and heartbeat that bound us together. In the Sichko household, my parents taught us the importance of getting together and worshiping with God's people. I embraced that idea and loved every moment of Mass.

I loved the incense on holy days. I loved statues and stained glass of Jesus, Mary, and Joseph. I loved the stories of the saints and martyrs. I loved going to Catholic school.

In third grade, we talked about what we wanted to be when we grew up. I raised my hand and said, "I want to be pope!"

Everyone laughed.

But, hey, if you think about it, I'm still in the running.

As a kid, I used to play priest. Honest truth. While other kids pretended to be baseball players or policemen, I handed out Pringles or Nilla Wafers, since, as you can guess, they're the closest objects I could find to the shape to the "Hosts" of communion.

My parishioner at the time, my dog Sheba, waited to be fed by the one speaking to her. Come to think of it, we're all a bit like that, being fed by the One speaking to us.

So, while I knew I wanted to be a priest early in life, something threatened to derail that call. As with most tempting things, the threat came from a good gift of God, my singing voice. The Devil is always at his best when he twists God's goodness for his own ends.

As a kid, my parents sent me to a local college for singing lessons. Everyone, from the nuns to my friends, told me my future would be in singing. I began to believe them and pushed myself. I dropped other commitments and focused on becoming a classically trained singer. Throughout school, I dedicated myself to the idea that I would bless the world with my voice.

Somewhere in the back of my head, I felt a nagging pull, a tug and even a little voice whisper, "I want you to be a priest."

I ignored those feelings and auditioned for the Boston University School of Music. Not only did the audition go well, but a member of the Tanglewood Summer Festival, summer home to the Boston Pops, sat in the audience. They offered me an opportunity to attend for the summer, a rare opportunity for an 18-year-old.

Imagine my pride, my excitement and crazy joy at the idea. All my hard work as a kid would finally pay off.

And, what a payoff! I sang with the Boston Pops. I babysat for Yo Yo Ma's son Nicholas. I grabbed a burger with the legendary Leonard Bernstein. As the kids in my youth group say, I was "living the dream."

In my family's home in Texas, my mom keeps framed posters of all the autographs I received that summer. Everyone gave me the nickname, "Autograph Hound Sichko." The posters, personalized to me, give testimony to that fantastic summer with names like Kiri Te Kanawa, Maestro Seiji Ozawa, Leonard Bernstein, and Pianist András Schiff.

All my creative cylinders fired that summer. Still, as I attended daily Mass at St. Ann's Catholic Church, located just blocks away from Tanglewood, I would kneel, pray, and receive the Eucharist, and not be able to shake the idea of being a priest.

In the end, I gave Boston University a pass and chose the New England Conservatory of Music. I majored in Vocal Performance and Opera, with some of the best teachers, coaches, and general education around. Everyone told me a worldwide classical career was in my future.

Yet, I hid a secret from everyone — a secret that I would share with no one, a secret that would have shocked all who knew me.

I started to research how I could use my singing gift in the Roman Catholic Priesthood. The desire to be a priest that always remained near the surface finally broke into the open.

On a hot July 4th, the Boston Pops practiced for their performance at Tanglewood. As a camper, they gave me an opportunity to sing a solo that night.

During the rehearsal, I think I kept missing my notes, cues, and intros. Finally, my voice teacher, a dignified lady with gray hair, asked me, "Jim, what do you want to do?"

"I... I just don't want to do this anymore."

She gave me a long, searching look.

"Well, what do you want then? Do you want another piece of music?"

I heard myself blurt out, "No, I don't want to sing! I want to be a priest. I want to serve God's people and preach the Word throughout the world."

She immediately responded, "Well, go and do it and stop wasting my time!"

This memory always cracks me up. God always uses strange things to get my attention, and I'm pretty convinced that the Holy Spirit used my voice teacher that summer day.

All of those memories ran through my head as I drove home from the retreat center. I had given up a possible world-famous singing career. I had given up all the respect and power that came with it.

In only a matter of minutes, I'd been dismissed from my dream of the priesthood.

God wouldn't let this happen . . . Would He?

Kneeling

When I got home, I sat on our couch, dazed and confused. The autograph wall seemed to mock me with my lost opportunity.

Dear God, did I miss You? Should I have just been a singer?

I looked at the phone and realized I needed to hear a supporting voice. Any voice, since God didn't seem to be speaking to me at the moment.

The first call went to my mom and sister. They'd gone on a shopping trip to Houston. Thankfully, they hadn't left the hotel room. (This was before cell phones, remember.)

"Mom, I…"

"Jimmy, what's wrong?"

"They kicked me out. I can't go back to seminary."

Silence.

"Mom? Are you there?"

"There has to be a mistake."

"No, Mom, I mean, maybe there was, I dunno. Father told me today."

"Jimmy, we're going to be home as soon as we can. Sit tight. I love you."

"I love you, too."

"Go next door to Barb and Don's."

"I will."

After I hung up, I did just that. I must've looked like a train wreck victim when I arrived at our neighbor's house. Barb and Don Ori, friends and family, gave me more tea and sympathy than I can remember. They took one look at me, brought me into their house and let me dump all my hurt on their living room table.

When I finished, they said, "So, what are you going to do?"

I know they asked the question out of genuine concern, but I honestly couldn't answer.

Don looked at me. "I mean, this isn't the final word, is it? Can't you fight it? Especially if you think Father was wrong?"

"I guess . . . I mean, what if Father and the diocese aren't wrong? What if I'm not supposed to be a priest?"

They both laughed and said, "Jimmy, if there is one person in this world called to be a priest, it's you. Figure out how you can appeal the decision and go from there."

I sat back on their couch and put my head in my hands. My friends didn't realize there would be no appeal process, at least with my home diocese. Still, there might be other ways forward, and I couldn't lose hope. God used my family and extended family to help me see the truth. If I believed God called me to the priesthood, I needed to find a way.

This is why I laugh at commercials that talk about "being your own person." If I believed advertising, I would still be moping in the corner, complaining to God about how He never speaks.

He does speak. All the time. Most often, it's through other people, their voices, mannerisms, and in their own way of saying things. It's the way He always moves, even when He wrote His own book, the Bible. He used the prophets, poets, apostles and others to speak to the whole world. He used their personalities and their shortcomings. That's the way He works.

Okay, God, I got it. I'm going to figure this out.

I went home and called my seminary spiritual director, Father Tony Ostini.

"Jim, how are you? Ready to come back?"

"Not exactly."

The light tone he answered the phone with stopped, and he went into "Confessor" mode.

"Jim, have you decided to give up being a priest?"

"Well, no, actually . . . my diocese told me I can't go back."

"What?"

I recounted the conversation at the retreat center.

"No, we can't let that happen. I won't let that happen. I'll do whatever I can. I'll get Sister Elizabeth to write a letter of support as well. She knows you well, right?"

"Yes, Father, she's been a mentor and a spiritual advisor, just like you."

"Good, then we'll get on it. You should probably call Dr. Rieveschl to help." I remained quiet as he rattled off advice. When I didn't say anything, he stopped and asked, "What's bothering you, Jim?"

"What if the Father is right? What if I shouldn't be a priest?"

"Don't you think I'd tell you if you shouldn't?"

"Would you?"

He laughed. "Jimmy, my boy, if I didn't think you were cut out to be a priest, I would have told you. We would have discerned this together. I can tell you without reservation I believe you should be a priest, so let me know if I can do more."

The next year and half developed into a time of learning humility. Think about it. Think about a dream you've pursued with all of your heart, soul, and mind. Everyone close to you and even those not close to you know about it. They are all supporting you, rooting for you, and interested in the progress of your dream.

Now, imagine that your dream failed in a sudden, spectacular, and unexpected way. Everyone, not knowing the circumstances, is asking you questions like, "Why aren't you at seminary? What happened to your desire to be a priest? Did you just give it up? Did you not have the calling, after all? Why would you want to serve a church that had wounded you so greatly? Do you have a martyr complex?"

I was asked all of those questions, believe it or not.

I couldn't help but wonder if those people thought things they didn't share with me, such as: "I bet he couldn't hack it. I bet he's just a flake who can't decide what he wants to do. He quit music, so let's just chalk this up to another failed attempt by Jim."

You know, it's amazing how much we can be locked in the jail of our own self-centeredness. We get so involved in our own self-pity and sadness. Pity parties are actually fun in a twisted, weird way. You know why? We're still at the center of everything. We're still the focus. And, in our broken and sinful hearts, we love the attention we get at the party.

This isn't to say we don't grieve when we experience a loss or rejection. The Bible is full of stories of people dealing with feeling abandoned. Read the Book of Job. Everyone knows the pain of being cast out or rejected. This sort of trial comes in many forms, such as the loss of a friendship, being fired from a job, the horror of a divorce, or the death of someone we love.

In these hard times, we need to be re-centered, rebooted, and stripped to the center of our lives. We need to find our way back to Christ Himself.

How did Our Lord reveal Himself to me and allow me to refocus? Very simply. I found what I needed at my local parish.

Night after night, I would walk to church. Usually, I sat by myself, kneeling in the chapel of the Blessed Sacrament. In the presence of Christ, I poured out my heart to Him. I asked for Jesus to examine me and show me what He wanted. I knew as I prayed that I needed to be open to the fact that God may send me in another direction.

Then, one night, I focused on the Blessed Sacrament and thought about everything the Eucharist represents to us. Catholics believe the Host and the Wine become the actual body and blood of Christ. This isn't cannibalism, as many of the early Romans thought; instead, it's a real, significant, and profound demonstration of Jesus being with us every moment of our lives.

The story of how we got the Eucharist is a pretty familiar one. The night before Jesus died on the cross, He held a meal with His disciples. At that meal, He used unleavened bread (part of the Jewish feast of Passover) and red wine to show His followers a new way, His way. He commanded His friends to do this at every church meal and He would be present with them always.

As I thought about the sacrament, I thought about Jesus being the central point of all history. Everything flowed to Him and through Him. Everything is about Him. This is why Catholics celebrate the Eucharist at the high point of Mass. It's the special, unique reminder that Jesus is with us – the center point of all human history connected to His people.

As these thoughts raced through my head, I went to my knees. I knew that I didn't serve the church, its people, its hierarchy, or even myself. I served the Living Lord, the reason for all beings and the Creator of all things.

The idea struck me hard and I knew at that moment I would be a priest. I knew I wanted to serve the Eucharist for the rest of my life so I could remind people that Christ is with us, in us, and moves through us. I wanted to serve the God who created each of us, and through His will, He would use me, as unworthy as I am to lead, to teach and sanctify. It is through that service that I would become an extension of my bishop to the people for which he is ultimately responsible.

When that realization sank in, I got up from my knees with a renewed determination to plan a different road to the priesthood.

I think the big problem in my home diocese is that those who oversaw my vocational studies believed that someone trained as a professional "performer" would "cease" performing and be a humble servant of God's people. I'm not sure I ever overcame that prejudice, and I knew no amount of support letters would change that perception.

The letters did come, though, which solidified the idea I should be a priest. Along with my spiritual mentors at the seminary, Dr. Jan Rieveschl, a well-respected psychologist in the church, sent a letter to combat the "performer" tag attached to me.

He wrote:

Given the productive and progressive tone of Mr. Sichko's work at the seminary, his dismissal (which was initiated by his diocese) came as a total and extremely puzzling surprise. Since the decision process was closed to Mr. Sichko, he was left almost completely in the dark as to the charges against him. He was availed of no opportunity to rebut the case against him, to call witnesses on his behalf, or to gather evidence with which to defend himself. I must say quite frankly that such total lack of due process within an otherwise Christian organization is ironic to say the least. The decision hit him like a bolt out of the blue. Based upon my experience with him, and promise within the seminary program, I could not and cannot find grounds for such an action.

Dr. Rieveschl's words made me feel confirmed in my call, but they fell on deaf ears.

I knew I had to find a job. I found one at a nearby Catholic school as a middle school Religion teacher. As I met the students, I couldn't help but enjoy their enthusiasm for the faith. I realized that whatever God wanted for my future, He wanted me to teach these kids about Him right now.

Those students kept me going, because at night, I would lie in my bed, crying out to God. I thumbed through vocation magazines and read about various communities who sought people to serve in the work of the church. I prayed over each and wondered where God wanted me.

While flipping through a Catholic Directory, I remember coming across the Coat of Arms of the Bishop of Lexington, Kentucky. The motto underneath the crest spoke directly to me: "Act Justly, Love Tenderly, Walk Humbly (Micah 6:8)." Could this bishop truly believe and mold his life after these powerful, yet humble words?

In a flurry, I grabbed a paper and pen. I sat at my desk in the calm of the night and wrote what was in my heart to the bishop: "I am willing to come to the Catholic Diocese of Lexington as a servant working for and with my brothers and sisters of Kentucky (Janitor,

Chaplain, Teacher – Servant, no less). It is my sincere prayer and hope that I will hear a positive response in the future. However, I continue to leave this all in God's Hands."

After a year and a half of being dismissed from my home diocese, the bishop approved my request to come for a one-year trial period through the Diocese of Lexington. As I flew to Kentucky, I couldn't focus as thoughts crowded into my brain. Would they welcome me? Would I get there and feel like this was all a huge mistake? Would they take one look at me, frown and say, "Get back on the plane, Jim."

When I got off the airplane, the Vocation Director at the time, Father William Brown, met me, shook my hand, and said, "Welcome, Jim." His warmness, kindness, and love made me feel this would be home. I realized how much I needed that feeling. I left behind my family and arrived with nothing but one suitcase.

However, I received something more important in return. The past year and a half had molded me. God used it to shape me by stripping away my ego and self-assuredness. He refined me into a ball of energy, revving (I have problems with going fast, as you'll see) to serve His people.

The bishop sent me to finish my studies at Sacred Heart Seminary in Hales Corner, Wisconsin. Finally, on May 23, 1998, after years of trials, sorrows, joys, and plain crazy things, I would be ordained.

I woke up that morning with my stomach doing backflips. As I got dressed, I thought about all the people who would be there to see me become a priest. I smiled when I thought about my former classmate, Patrick Bolton, who would be in the congregation.

Patrick came from deep Irish Catholic roots. He stood six-foot-five with flaming-red hair. We became best friends during our studies despite the fact he is a morning person and I'm not.

I would stumble into the darkened seminary chapel each morning at 7 a.m. for Morning Prayer. As I glanced over at Patrick he would grin at me. I put my head back down and would grumble to God, "Lord, are you sure you called Patrick to ordained ministry?"

When I arrived at the Cathedral at 10:25 a.m., just five minutes before I would be ordained to the Ministerial Priesthood of Jesus Christ, Patrick waited for me. I couldn't be more excited because we'd not seen each other since that infamous Christmas break. He opened the door, hugged me, and said, "I've got something to tell you."

Curious, I followed him to a quiet place and asked, "What's this about?"

Patrick smiled as he said, "Jim, do you remember all those days when we would come into Morning Prayer, you would glance over at me, I would smile and you would just lower your head? Do you remember?"

I chuckled. "Of course I remember, but why do you ask?"

"Well Jim," he replied, "It was at that time I would ask God if He was sure you were being called to priesthood!"

I busted up laughing. "You know, I thought the same about you!"

Turns out, Patrick felt a different call. He met a wonderful woman; they got married and had two beautiful kids. He became a father, too, just in a different way.

If you've never seen an ordination liturgy, you should. I love the beauty, the Mass, the Eucharist and the laying on of hands by the bishop.

As I bent the knee to be ordained, I thought about the hands ordaining me, and the hands that ordained them. I thought about how far that chain of hands went, even all the way back to the gnarled, fishermen hands of the apostles. Each hand a different color, attached to a different person, but all dedicated to the same Lord and the same church.

I looked back to realize how much God prepared every step of the way. He used my music skills so I might sing at Mass and lead people into worship. He used my gift of speaking, presence, and structure to preach sermons to the people of God.

So now, fifteen years later, I write this as I look out on my second family's farm, Robindale, in Kentucky. I smile because of the life the Lord has given me. I get to serve Him as a priest, the same Jesus who reached out to those who were outcast and "dismissed" by society; the same Jesus who reached out to me, once "dismissed," now active in spreading and living His word among us. What a wonderful journey it is . . . and will be.

Stories

I love stories. I'm thinking I'm not alone in that, either. Billions of dollars are spent on novels, movies, and even video games. Why? God made us to function through story. Not only did He reveal Himself in the greatest-selling Book of all time, but He made story a vital part of how we communicate with each other.

Think about it. We are a storytelling people. From the moment we are born, growing up through school and beyond, we love hearing stories being read and told to us. We love sharing experiences that we have lived, seen, or heard. For me, as a storyteller, preacher, and speaker, stories provide the opportunity to communicate in a powerful way with people in everyday language with down-to-earth tales.

I think back to my own days at St. Mary Catholic School in kindergarten and how we loved to sit in a circle and listen to Mrs. Richard read to us. We learned from the plot, the characters, and their actions. She read with a passion and belief that captivated our little minds. Most importantly, the stories struck at our hearts.

Why do you think Jesus told stories to make His point? Indeed,

He is a master storyteller in all of His parables found in the four Gospels. He would use everyday situations that people understood. He used characters that people would recognize in themselves and others. Even more interesting, Jesus didn't always provide the answers. He let people figure out His meaning by telling them, "He who has ears, let them hear."

God gave me a very interesting life story, as you're going to see throughout this book. I like to think He gave me this life so I could tell stories from my journey. As you might guess, when I travel to speak at different places, I am often asked two questions. First, "Are your stories true?" and, second, "How do these experiences always happen to you?"

My answer is simple: Yes, the stories are true, and yes, they do happen to me, and they happen to you! The real question that needs to be asked is, "Do you and I have the eyes, the ears, and the hearts — not to mention the minds — to recognize the wonderful opportunities and teachable moments from the experiences of our day?"

Through sorrow, pain, joys, and exultations, our experiences teach us; they stretch us. For me, stories empower and illumine the life of Our God who is ever present with us on this journey through our experiences that we call "Life."

Allow me to tell you a few...

Hollywood – Among Friends

Ten years ago, my bishop assigned me to be the pastor at St. Mark Catholic Church in Richmond, Kentucky. I arrived to find the church paying off a huge debt with no end in sight. We talked about various ways to solve our problem and relieve the burden of the church.

As Catholics reading this book can imagine, we tried all the old standbys for parishes all over the world. We tried ice cream socials. We tried pancake breakfasts. Yes, we did the legendary Catholic bingo. None of it really made a dent.

One night, I woke up with a crazy, amazing idea. I would contact a celebrity and extend an invitation to St. Mark's for a huge party. We could charge an admission fee, take part of it to pay off the debt, and then put the rest toward a local charity.

Presto. Everyone would love this idea and get in line. Brilliant, right?

Well, not quite.

As you can imagine, people brought quite a few legitimate questions.

They asked, "Why would a celebrity come to Richmond, Kentucky? Why would we even want to give part of the money away, isn't this to help us and not others? Could this even be possible?"

All good questions, and I realized to get this done, I would need to do a lot of convincing.

I told people that sometimes to achieve something, you've gotta go big or go home. Everyone understood this point, to their credit. Then, I said, celebrities will most likely come if we give part of the proceeds to a charity.

Live with Regis

After a few conversations with people in the church, we decided to extend an invitation to Regis Philbin. I did a crazy amount of research, called in a few favors, yanked on a few strings, and finally connected with Regis. He agreed to come to our little parish.

Despite what I said to my congregation, I couldn't believe it. Regis would come to our church. When I announced the visit, another list of questions came up. "Why would I want to spend money to see Regis? What is he going to do?"

Let me tell you, those questions caused me a few sleepless nights. Yes, Regis was great on TV, but what would he do with a live audience? Quiz them like he did contestants on Who Wants to be a Millionaire? What would convince people to come see him?

Turns out, everyone wanted to come. We sold out the tickets and people begged for more. Regis's requirements for travel turned out to be very minimal, and God provided for his needs. My good friends, Dr. and Mrs. Bennett, agreed to host the event at their home and well-known international caterer Jerry Lundergan agreed to provide the food.

The day of the event arrived and I went to Cincinnati to pick up Regis. I got to greet him right on the tarmac (prior to 9/11).

"Father, I love your crazy idea," he said as he shook my hand. Then, Regis noticed everyone waiting to talk to him.

"Ah, excuse me, Father; want to say hi to all these folks."

I watched as he signed autographs, took pictures, and made everyone laugh. I reflected on how the simple thing of saying hello and talking with people made their day. Sure, Regis isn't God, nor did he pretend to be a big-deal celebrity. He just wanted to make everyone smile.

He is the real deal.

When we got to Richmond, he wanted to talk to the kids at our school. We organized a meet and greet. Regis talked to the students about hard work, getting an education, and determination. He told stories about how he worked his way up through the entertainment industry. The kids loved him. Our local TV station did a remote report. He got the kids involved and the media loved it.

Later that evening, Regis dined in the middle of over 500 people under a tent in Richmond, Kentucky. He sat with my mother, sister, bishop, Dr. and Mrs. Bennett, and me. We laughed, ate, and told stories. The meal became more of a family dinner than a celebrity event.

A bit nervous, I got up and said, "Okay folks, so here is the crazy idea, and it worked! Y'all know this man and what he does, so I don't need to tell you. Without further ado, Regis Philbin!"

Everyone clapped and applauded. He gave a great talk on his career and his faith. Then, he decided to sing a few numbers. As he started to wrap up, he looked at me and said, "Father, I know you can sing. Come on up."

I joined him and said, "What shall we sing?"

"Well, I know you're Italian, but I thought we could sing a song of my people, the Irish."

So, we launched into the Irish lullaby, "Too Ra Loo Ra Loo Ral." For the finale, the band started to play the "Notre Dame Victory March" as we made our way through the tent toward the Bennett house.

People ask me about Regis's faith. There is no doubt he is Catholic. Although I'm not sure if he attends Mass on a regular basis, I can say a few things. First, the man I saw glowed with Christ in the way he treated people and talked to the children. Each time I went to New York, he invited me to Live! with Regis and Kelly. After the show, we'd hang out in his office full of Notre Dame memorabilia. This man treated people as Christ treated people, and still does.

Jell-O Pudding

The next celebrity evening, we landed Bill Cosby. Unlike Regis, Mr. Cosby travels in his own jet with the label of "Billy" on the side. In order to pick him up, I needed to get to the airport in the middle of the night. I kept myself busy until I noticed the clock.

Yikes, I thought, I'm late.

I threw on some old clothes, got in the car and sped to the airport. By the time I got there, his plane had landed and started to roll into the private terminal.

So, Bill Cosby arrived in the middle of the night, I forgot to wear my clericals, and I got to the airport late.

Each of these celebrities, just like normal people, has their own moods and styles. As Mr. Cosby's plane stopped in the terminal, he deplaned and I stayed in my spot, waiting for an opportunity to greet him.

I noticed that Mr. Cosby went behind the tail of the plane and retrieved his own luggage. In my rush to help him, I approached and said, "Mr. Cosby, can I get that for you?"

He brushed me off and said, "It's too late." The comedian got into a waiting vehicle without another word.

I felt bad and didn't know what to say. I couldn't figure out what I did wrong.

The next morning, I waited eagerly at the church for Mr. Cosby's car to show. When it did, I leaned into the window and asked the driver to pop the trunk so I could retrieve the luggage.

"Now, Father, you really don't have to do that. I told you that last night."

I shook him off. "Mr. Cosby, you may not have realized, but last night I did not show you the proper hospitality that we here at St. Mark and in the great state of Kentucky are known for. If you remember, I was 'too late' according to you in retrieving your luggage from the plane. But today, I'm right on time!"

He laughed, hugged my neck, and gave me that Cosby smile. As he rolled his eyes, he said, "Let's eat."

At the concert, everyone laughed so hard they couldn't see straight. I thought I might need to give my bishop an infusion of oxygen after Mr. Cosby talked about "a visit to the dentist."

In one routine, he discussed finding out about Catholics while growing up in a Protestant household. He said, "You know, I always considered Catholics the 'quiet people.' They could make their point to God without all of the shouting and carrying on we did at our church."

Everyone laughed as he continued. "Plus, I could never understand the prayers because they were all in Latin. Of course, I realized, I didn't understand my grandfather's prayers either. I told him that once and my grandfather said, 'Well, Bill, I'm not talking to you.'"

Everyone roared.

In between the performances, the comedian developed an eye problem. Thankfully, we found him a specialist: Dr. Osentinsky, a noted Otolaryngologist. Dr. Osentinsky arrived and assisted Mr. Cosby in his trailer. Mr. Cosby insisted that I stay with him during the examination. I remember a month or so later that Dr. Osentinsky received a note of thanks from the legendary Mr. Cosby.

After the treatment, he got up and gave a fantastic performance. How he did it, I'm not sure, but he gave credit to the idea, "The show must go on."

Fame Becomes Me

The comedy concert turned out so well, we decided to host another one. This time, we chose Howie Mandel. Everything seemed well in hand, and we couldn't wait to have him.

However, as the months passed, his staff became concerned about performing in a church space. Further, they went fifteen rounds over a clause in the contract when I stipulated that Mr. Mandel couldn't use offensive language during his routine.

Finally, he cancelled and I didn't understand it. Why does he need bad language to be funny? It just didn't make sense to me.

As it turned out, God gave us someone better suited for our crowd: Martin Short.

I couldn't get over the difference in working with him. He submitted his material to me, to make sure it would be okay.

On the night of the performance, I got up to do my usual introduction.

"Ladies and gentlemen, this is one of the funniest men I've ever met in my life. He's been gracious and awesome, and I can't wait for you to meet him. Mr. Martin Short!"

The crowd rose up and applauded as loud as they could as Martin came out on stage.

He bowed and then shouted, "Please, please, please be seated. You don't know how this makes a big star like me feel, especially since I was Father Jim's second choice!"

Immediately the crowd roared with laughter and gave Martin another standing ovation.

He launched into an amazing performance where he did voices, changed costumes for different characters, and even sang some hilarious songs. In one particular skit, he dressed up as his famous character, Jiminy Glick.

Glick is a heavyset talk show host who insults his guests through his rudeness. When Martin did his character on Comedy Central, he interviewed the likes of Steve Martin, Jerry Seinfeld, and Tom Hanks.

His celebrity guest for this night? Me.

Martin brought me on stage and began the interview.

"You're in wonderful shape for someone who's let himself go."

The audience roared, and I laughed.

"Thanks, Jiminy, you as well."

"Now, I want to know a little about your journey, but not too much, because I'm really just pretending to care."

More laughter.

The night continued with great success, and Martin concluded by talking about his charity work and how he loved this sort of event.

Unforgettable

So, we had hosted two comedians and a media personality with great success. I wanted to mix things up a bit. To do so, I went with my music background. After getting some feedback from church members, I decided to invite Natalie Cole.

When I met her at the airport, she greeted me with a warm smile and said, "Father, I didn't expect you to pick me up."

I smiled and asked, "Why not? I enjoy doing it."

We talked on our way to baggage claim, and her personal assistant and I started to remove trunk after trunk of luggage.

I leaned over to the assistant and said, "We already got all the sound equipment, we didn't really need all this."

The assistant smiled. "Oh, it's not sound equipment, Father, this is Natalie's wardrobe."

I scratched my head. "But, she's only doing two shows in one day."

She laughed. "Father, she's gotta have choices."

When we got to the church, she decided to go right into rehearsal. Keep in mind, I'd never heard any of her music and I couldn't wait to hear her voice.

The moment she opened her mouth, I started to tear up. Her voice filled me with awe, beauty, and love. The passion she put into every word just astounded me.

Natalie entranced the crowd that night. When she sang "Mary, Did You Know?" it brought the house down. Everyone gave her a five-minute standing ovation.

When the concert finished, I announced our next guest for Among Friends. Natalie came out in her bunny slippers and peeked through the curtains.

I asked, "Ms. Cole, are you going to do another song for us?"

She said, "No, I just wanted to hear who you were bringing in next."

Everyone laughed and applauded.

All of these concerts take place in the sanctuary of our church. It only holds 500 people, and the performances have a really intimate feel. Most of these performers could pack arenas, so the fact we got them to come to such a small venue was a true blessing.

The people of St. Mark really connected with Natalie. Immediately after she left, it was reported in the news that she came down with a serious illness which would require some lengthy treatment and a transplant. I kept in touch with Natalie, and our St. Mark community showered her with many prayers, keeping vigil with her through it all. In fact, privately, with only my secretary knowing at the time, I corresponded with the transplant team in California to see if I was a "match" to assist Ms. Cole with her medical needs.

Rebounding as she did, and overcoming these health issues, we invited Natalie back to St. Mark. She was the only performer at that time to be invited for a "second go-round." Even though she was still regaining her stamina, she seemed much more relaxed and comfortable during her second visit to St. Mark. Everyone loved her.

Workin' 9 to 5

Next, I landed what I believed was one of the biggest "coups" of all: the agreement of Dolly Parton to play St. Mark's An Evening Among Friends. It was after much writing, finagling, and pestering Dolly's personal Manager, Danny Nozell (who has become a very close personal friend of mine and our church), that she agreed to come to St. Mark, even arranging her fall tour around our event.

As expected, Dolly was Dolly! Her entire performance extended over two hours with no intermission or costume change. Dolly shared her life story with us. In fact, my bishop leaned over to me and said he felt he "was at church" with the religious overtones of the entire performance.

Dolly's visit developed into our first experience with groupies. From the moment that Dolly's performance was announced at St. Mark, we began receiving requests for tickets from all over the world. England, Scotland, Canada, Mexico, not to mention people sending cakes, flowers, and mementos to be signed.

That evening, when I got up to introduce Dolly, I gave her a rousing introduction that made her say, "Father, you sounded like a Pentecostal preacher, not a Catholic priest!"

Of course, everyone loved that.

Then, she told a story about her very large family. She said, "People ask me if my family was Catholic. I say, 'Naw, just overly fertile hillbillies.'"

She belted out song after song, including a gospel tune that got everyone up and clapping to the beat. Needless to say, she rocked the church.

Speaking privately with Dolly during her visit, I asked her about the cake that I held from one of her fans.

Hoping that she would tell me that I could eat it, she immediately quipped, "Give it to me, we will put it on the bus and enjoy it!"

What's My Code Name?

I decided to take a new direction. Instead of An Evening Among Friends, I decided to go for A Day Among Friends. Our first speaker, former First Lady Laura Bush, would help us develop the new format.

Talk about a bizarre contrast. We went from dealing with Dolly's groupies to dealing with the Secret Service. I'm amazed at all the planning it takes for a former first lady to speak at an event. The agents did background checks, a complete inspection of St. Mark, and had code names for everyone involved.

I made this a running joke during the luncheon. When I introduced her, I said, "Mrs. Bush just won't tell me my Secret Service code name."

I'm guessing it might have been something like "Crazy Priest."

The former first lady showed her graciousness from the moment I flew with her on her private plane from Dallas until she departed to return home.

One of my greatest memories with Mrs. Bush was the opportunity she provided for our school. She met with the students, read to them, and visited with each one before heading out to Dr. and Mrs. Kessler's residence, where our luncheon was held. It was a great day not only for St. Mark, but I believe for Kentucky as well.

I remember telling Mrs. Bush that all of the events I hosted at St. Mark were catered by Jerry Lundergan, a longtime Democrat and personal friend of the Clintons. Mr. Lundergan, who is also a close friend of my family, has catered inaugurations, the Olympics, and

NASCAR events, and fed thousands upon thousands of people when natural disasters have struck our country.

Immediately, as we were heading to the tent to speak, Mr. Lundergan happened to be off to the side, and I alerted her of his presence. She went over and thanked Jerry for his time and they spent a few minutes in conversation. I loved seeing a Republican and Democrat getting along, even for just a few moments.

Who Dat?

We decided to go back to a music theme for Among Friends, so we chose to bring in Harry Connick, Jr. as our next celebrity guest. Harry, who radiates with warmth, humor, passion, and the zest of New Orleans, brought down the church not only once but twice – and we'd love to have him for a third time as well. The team around Harry, including his band and tour/office staff, are amazing. Harry and my mother, whom he has named "Miss Marie," formed a very strong bond.

My mother simply adores Harry. In fact, on his second appearance to St. Mark, I shared with the audience a recent conversation that I'd had with him.

"Harry, I'm a bit concerned about something."

He furrowed his eyebrows and said, "What's that, Father?"

I pursed my lips and shook my head. "As a son, I've gotta say, I'm a bit concerned about your connection with my mother. What are your intentions? Do you intend to marry her?"

Harry burst out laughing and said, "Then you would have to call me Father, Father!"

Everyone in the crowd lost it.

Through our relationship with Harry, our parish became united with Musicians' Village in New Orleans. It is a wonderful place located in the 9th Ward that provides music lessons, performance space, and opportunities for those who might not otherwise have such a chance.

Our parish has provided Musicians' Village (and Mountain Mission School) with over 500 pounds of new toys at Christmas, as well as Easter baskets, with the hopes of offering our college students an "alternative" spring break of service opportunities over boozing adventures.

One of the great things about the Harry Connick, Jr. event is the present bishop of Beaumont, my old diocese, flew up as my personal guest. He stayed with me at my house and we had wonderful conversations. I reflected on the fact that God began the process of bringing restoration through Among Friends. What started off as a journey of personal anger and frustration ended with the beauty of gospel transformation.

I'm A Little Bit Rock 'n Roll

Finally, last December, we hosted entertainer Donny Osmond. I think Donny's performance was the most energized of all, and he truly lived up to the reputation of being a "showman."

As I introduced his name to the audience, everyone jumped to their feet. Donny surprised the crowd by entering from the rear of the church and was greeted by loud screams and applause. Next to Dolly, Donny brought a huge line of groupies who came to St. Mark from all over the United States.

As the college students and I were loading in the morning of the concerts, a member of our church came to me and said there were three women at the back door waiting to enter for the concert.

I exclaimed, "What?! It's 7:30 in the morning and the concert is not until 5 o'clock! Let me go and see."

I walked down the hall to the back door and, sure enough, there were three women, two from California and another from Washington state.

"Ladies, can I help you?"

"Oh, we go from state to state following Donny. We're waiting for the best possible seats."

"Well, how are you going to eat? You should really go back to your hotel, do some sightseeing and enjoy Kentucky."

"Oh, no, we couldn't do that. We've got to say."

"Ladies, I promise you, I'll save you the best seats, never fear."

As I didn't have my clericals on, they asked, "And who are you, sir?"

I couldn't help but joke with them. "I'm just a hired hand, but I know all the right people."

They each shook their head and said, "We will wait."

I shrugged my shoulders and let them.

When I came back later in my clericals, I escorted them personally to front row center. I then wondered if my CPR skills would be needed.

Another unique aspect of Donny's visit to our Roman Catholic Church of St. Mark is that Donny is a member of the Church of Jesus Christ of Latter Day Saints. As you can expect, I got a lot of criticism over having a Mormon sing in our sacred space.

What most people didn't understand is that we conceived all of this as a fundraiser, not an evangelical mission for the church. Plus, through the celebrities, we got people into the church who would have thought twice about going into a Catholic sanctuary.

For me, the Among Friends idea is about teaching the importance of giving and receiving. Through a portion of our proceeds, we've helped support numerous charities such as the YMCA, Ennis Cosby Scholarship Fund, Hope's Wing's Domestic Violence Program, Karyn Kuhn Yates Scholarship Fund, Imagination Library, Musicians' Village, National Breast Cancer Awareness Fund, etc.

Yet, this event is more than just a fundraiser. It's about breaking down walls, introducing new friends, and developing long-lasting relationships. I'm often amazed at how people who may never get along in the "real world" find themselves bound together by mutual loves.

To me, that's how God works. His ways are not our ways. He reserves the right to act in ways we might find offensive. For example, He used the Wise Men's knowledge of astrology to guide them to Christ. Do I approve of that? No, but then I'm not God.

I worked behind the scenes with the mission president of the Mormon missionaries to bring some of them to Donny's concert as a gift from St. Mark Catholic Church. These 18- and 19-year-old missionaries of the Mormon Church give up two years of their lives to preach the Good News of Jesus Christ. They leave home and become "evangelizers" of their faith and their message. It was an awesome sight to see over 60 missionaries arrive at our church and be greeted with warmth, hospitality, and excitement. Many of them shared that this was their first ever visit to a Catholic Church, and it was interesting to see some of them seem quite suspicious or intrigued by their visit.

At the end of the concert, I asked for everyone to depart the church except for the missionaries who were present. I then shared how I remembered missionaries visiting my home when I was a youngster on many occasions and how I respected their goodness to me and my family. I also shared how I thought it was interesting that the missionaries always showed up at my home around dinner time – as word got around that my mom was a great Italian cook!

Finally, I mentioned that each time they would visit our household, they would leave a copy of the Book of Mormon. All the missionaries laughed. With sincerity, I then shared with them that I would like to give them something: a copy of the Catechism of the Catholic Church. I wished for them to read and reflect upon it, not to convert them, but to help them and us communicate and get to know one another better.

Immediately after that, as a surprise, Donny came out and visited with the missionaries, who at a moment's notice got up to serenade us with their mission song. That was the best sign I know, or have seen, that represents the powerful grace of Ecumenism.

———

So, why do I do all of this?

As I said, we do it for the parish and the charities. But, as we go along, the friends we meet through the experience give us a new dimension to keep going. I start seeing how God moves in so many ways through so many different people. I love to see the laughter, the food, the talking, and everyone's walls come down at these events, which still continue on an annual basis.

Of course, none of this could be achieved without the great support and energy of the St. Mark staff, family, friends, and the diocese. I am especially indebted to my oldest brother, Bill, and his wife, Sherre, who through their financial generosity, along with that of their colleagues, have always been there to help in my time of need.

We learn through all of these events that God uses all ways — contemporary, traditional, and unusual — to spread the message. We aren't the message, but we are messengers, nonetheless.

Those who have ears, let them hear.

T.R.U.S.T

Mornings and I are not friends. In fact, I'm convinced God uses them as penance in my life. While most Catholic parishes have early morning Mass, mine doesn't. I rescheduled our daily Mass to 6 p.m. Why? Because I'm not sure how holy I feel too early in the morning.

It's also why I love Midnight Mass.

Anyway, the irony of all this is that I'm often called to take morning flights in my travels. On one particular occasion, I woke up early in New York City for a flight to Orlando. When I say "early," I don't mean "Father Jim early" (which is eight in the morning). No, it was "5 a.m. early."

I rushed to get to the airport, went through security, and joined the line to board the plane. Inside the aircraft, I found my usual seat, the emergency exit window. As I sat there waiting for the plane to take off, I did what everyone else does: I examined the people coming down the aisle. I want to know who is sitting next to me, and if that person will be a huge, chattering pain. I'm not up for much conversation that hour of the morning. (I'm a priest, so you can't lie to me; you know you do it, too.) It is important to note that on this particular day, I dressed in my clericals, which scream "THIS MAN IS A PRIEST."

As I watched the line of people filter in, I saw a 93-year-old woman shuffling down the aisle. My heart sank as I prayed to God in an honest way, "Dear Lord, please don't do this to me. You know I am not a morning person. I don't even know if You are awake at this hour. Please, Lord, these individuals are always attracted to me. Help her find another seat, through Christ Our Lord, Amen."

I made the Sign of the Cross, ending my prayer, and behold, the woman sat down right next to me.

As soon as she did, she turned to me and tapped my shoulder to get my attention. Of course, she already had it. She said, "Excuse me, Father, but you're in the wrong seat."

I just kind of leaned over and gave her that look. You know the look — rolling of the eyes, glare, etc. I turned toward the window and went back to my prayers.

A few minutes later, I felt another tap on my shoulder; this time more insistent. The woman exclaimed, "Father, excuse me, but you're in the wrong seat!"

I looked at her and said, "Ma'am, I travel all the time. This is my seat. I sit here all the time. 12A, emergency exit window. Now, you say your prayers, and I'll say mine — God bless you."

The engines began to power up as the pilot readied the aircraft for takeoff. All of a sudden, this little Italian woman unbuckles her seat belt and hits the flight attendant button.

Now, if you know anything about the FAA, everything — and I mean everything — has to come to a halt under this circumstance. Everyone, mostly business people with places to be and deadlines to meet, craned their necks to see what was going on. All of the flight attendants came running to this little woman sitting next to me. Their faces were full of concern as they were probably afraid she might be having a heart attack.

They nearly screamed, "Can we help you?!"

The little old woman smiled and said, "Oh yes, you see, Father wants to move. He can't sit by me."

I felt the glares from the business people throughout the plane. Everyone seemed to be muttering under their breath, wondering why a priest couldn't sit next to a nice old lady. I shrank bank into my seat, feeling about six inches tall. In the back of my brain, I wondered if I could find an exit from this hollow tube and die right on the spot.

The flight attendants looked at each other and asked her in very kind tone, "Why? Why does Father want to move?"

I put my hand over my eyes and kicked myself in silence.

Good job, Jimmy. If you'd been nice and not so arrogantly lost in your own little world, you could have resolved this without all the drama.

The tiny woman in the seat next to me looked up with all sincerity and said, "I just finished praying a Novena (which is nine days of prayer) this morning. And it says that, at the hour of my death, a priest would be present..."

Everyone hid their laughter as I unbuckled my seat belt, and up I went to the back of the plane.

I sat in 23E and reflected upon the experience as the plane took off. After I prayed for God's forgiveness for my surly morning attitude, I realized what a valuable lesson this woman had taught me. She trusted in God and believed what she prayed. Belief, faith, and prayer are very powerful characteristics and gifts of the Holy Spirit. There is a unique strength derived from such people, and it doesn't matter whether it comes from a 93-year-old woman, from a child, or from you or me.

Jesus challenges all of us from Scripture to realize and to recognize that God is Spirit. Those who worship God (i.e., you and I) "must worship God in spirit and truth." According to Scripture, trusting in God is the source of blessings in our lives. Most importantly, it is the source of great spiritual blessings. The person who trusts in the Lord will possess an inner strength that others will never have. There is a rootedness, a foundation, a belief, for those who have faith and trust in God when they pray.

So much so, they can stop an airplane and ask a priest to move from his seat.

You know them, and I know them. They're the people who use God as more than a 911 number. People who are rooted in faith have that determination, that commitment.

I see it every Sunday at Mass or at the end of one of my talks. People come up to me with looks of concern, sorrow, or trouble. They are undergoing some great strain in their lives from family problems, a loss of a job, or the loss of a loved one.

People come up to me and ask, "Father, may I see you for a moment?"

That doesn't seem like a huge statement of faith, but it is. Why? Well, the obvious answer would be, "Jim, you're a priest, of course they come to you, you represent God and they need your connection to him in their time of trouble."

Well, sort of.

In reality, they hear my stories about my mom, who possesses the true direct line to God. They make me promise to ask her to pray for them. No different than what those at the Wedding of Cana did when they experienced a traumatic situation of running out of wine at the reception. To avoid embarrassment, and knowing that Jesus was in attendance, they turned to the person who they knew could get something done in a moment: Mary, the Mother of Jesus.

In typical fashion, she (and my own mother) directs us all to Jesus. People of faith accept the trials that come their way. They don't run from God, but to God. If we are going to be honest with ourselves, one of the reasons we really don't trust God is because we really do not know God.

Relationships are built on knowing the other person. Most of us don't really know God and so we stand back from Him. We've got all the wrong pictures in our head given to us by either well-meaning church people or popular culture.

Have you ever uttered any of these lines, or heard them spoken to you?

"God helps those who help themselves."

"God is an angry judge waiting for you to mess up so He can whack you for it."

"God wants you to get it together and stop whining."

Who wants to know a person like that? No one, and that's why most people avoid God. They have so many wrong ideas and wrong notions about Him. As you can expect, that makes us not trust Him.

In reality, we've got to see that God displayed His trustworthiness through Jesus – who is God in the flesh. He came to earth to identify with us, to be with us, and to suffer with us. He understands us fully.

A few years ago, Joan Osborne asked this question in a popular song: "What if God was one of us?"

I answer: He was and He is. He understands not just because He made us, but because He did become one of us. If you're one of those people who say, "Trust has to be earned," well, God earned it through His son.

So, how does that work out in our lives? I make a little acronym to talk about just how that might look.

T.R.U.S.T

And it starts with Time...

T — Time

I call my mom three times a day.

I call her at 8 a.m. "Mom, what are you doing?"

"I'm praying."

I call her at noon, and I say, "Mom, what are you doing?"

"I'm praying."

I call her at 5 p.m. "Mom, what are you doing?"

"I'm cooking. Then I'm going to pray."

You may say that my mom has nothing to do, but have you ever prayed 24/7? It takes a lot of work and dedication. People who dedicate their lives to prayer do it for the benefit of others, not just for themselves.

Why do you think we have monasteries and cloistered convents throughout the world? Is it because they hate the world and just want to get away? No, they could go to the beach or live as hermits in the mountains somewhere. These holy men and women are dedicated to praying for you and me — for those of us who don't take the time out to pray.

I love visiting the Cloistered Dominican Nuns of Lufkin, Texas. Nestled away in the piney woods of East Texas is a monastery of holy women devoted to prayer. Any time, day or night, one can find at least one of the sisters praying before the Blessed Sacrament in the Chapel. Their usual intentions are for you and me. The Sisters don't have to know us by name, for God knows what we need even before we ask. The primary vocation for these sisters is to pray in adoration and to intercede on behalf of our needs, concerns, and sorrows.

Still, while it is comforting to know these beautiful people are praying for you, God wants your time, too. He wants to talk to you and about you. I always find it interesting when people tell me they don't feel holy enough to talk to God, as if any of us do. If you wait to become magically holy enough for God so that you can pray, I'm afraid you'll be waiting an eternity.

God doesn't want you to act holy when you come to Him. He just wants you to come to Him. He wants you to bring all of your sins, all of your mess, and all your filthy rags to lay at His feet. Prayer begins with you saying, "God, I'm not holy enough, but I love You. Here is all that I have."

If we are really seeking to acknowledge God in His divine presence, then we have to spend a great deal of time getting to know God. There is no other way. This is why daily prayer time is absolutely essential. Aside from Mass — the primary place where we get to know Our Lord — we have to spend time throughout our day conversing with the One who loves us, who is there for us, and who never abandons us.

The fact is that we have a deep trust only when we have a deep relationship with someone. And relationship is the "R" in "T.R.U.S.T."

R — Relationship

Let me tell you about the Sichko family, can I? You get all of us together for dinner, and this is how we function.

You ready?

We sit down and pass around the wine. Usually it's my older

brother Billy who takes center stage in telling a highlight of the day, story, or joke.

We eat and we talk. We talk loudly. We're animated, hands flying up in the air, faces pulled in exaggerated expressions.

Then plates start to fly.

And the napkins, spoons, and forks, too.

That's because we get emotional over what we're conversing about, and we must express ourselves with passion.

And then we bring out the second course, the pasta, and we begin to eat again. We resume talking, but all at the same time, overlapping each other in about eight different conversations. We start getting upset and storm off to our own different parts of the house. Mom brings out the chicken and brings us back to the table. We start talking again and the fight is forgotten.

You see, that's how family really works. Even in the midst of our screaming, talking, and pointing fingers, we understand that this is a part of who we are as a family. If we denied this, we would deny our very selves.

In fact, this is probably how Jesus and the disciples functioned. Most people have an overly "holy" view of how things worked in the Gospels. I think they imagined some emaciated, weak Jesus who whispered his wise sayings in a breathy "emo" voice. In fact, we're told in the Gospels that Jesus and His disciples looked pretty much like my family dinners. John and James schemed to get places at Jesus' side. Peter made bold declarations and then had to eat his words just a few minutes later.

Indeed, the church itself throughout its long history has been one big family fight and make-up dinner known as the Eucharist. This family meal is the center part of our church life not only because we meet Christ there, but we meet each other. It's where all relationships deepen and are strengthened. In the meal, and in our conversation with God, we find our relationships grow stronger.

You have to have relationships, because if you don't have relationships, you're not going to have family. The good, the bad, the indifferent — through all times, we communicate. We share with each other and get to know one other and what is going on in our lives.

When is the last time you truly conversed with those closest to you in your life? And I mean really conversed.

Get past the weather, taxes, soccer practice, and small talk to ask, "How are you doing?" And really mean it. Care about the answer. Be emotionally invested in the response. Such questions open the door to our souls. Knock on the door of those you love. And in return, leave a welcome mat on your own door for others to approach you.

Having that, you build relationships. You create family. This is one reason why Scripture reading is so important. It's not so much about reading the word of God as it is about obeying the word of God. As I tell my parishioners, "If your Bible is in good shape, you aren't!"

When we read Scripture and reflect on it, God speaks to us! He reveals Himself to us. It is God's spoken Word written for us. Scripture is God's way of being the ultimate storyteller to us, His children. And you know, sadly, this is the missing element in the prayer lives of many people. We have no trouble talking to God, but we never stop to listen to God. It's a give and take. No relationship will grow unless both sides speak and listen.

Even at chaotic family dinners.

I challenge people daily: "Put your expectations on God. Not on people. Form a relationship with God. Stop treating God badly with your one sided conversations. Let Him speak. He's got a lot to stay to you."

When the Lord speaks and we listen, our understanding increases. Understanding is the "U" in T.R.U.S.T!

U — Understanding

If we are going to trust God deeply, then we need to understand how God operates. One of the reasons I speak so freely about my mom is that I understand how my mom operates.

Several years ago, my mother called and had me fly down to be with her and my sister. She wanted us to have a little bonding experience, so she registered us for a CPR class at the American Red Cross. So here we were, all day, at the Red Cross, taking CPR lessons as a "bonding experience."

Immediately, after we passed the test, being Italians as we are, and being December 20th as it was, we killed two birds with one stone. And, as Italians, we celebrate how?

By eating.

So we went to the food court at the local mall. Have you ever been to the mall on December 20th?

Mamma mia.

So, my 4-foot-8-inch mom walked into the food court and noticed a man lying on the ground, with a crowd of people gathered around him. She took off like I have never seen an 85-year-old woman run.

My mom screamed, waving her ID card, "I have just been certified in CPR!"

She broke through the crowd, landed on top of the man, and began chest compressions.

Immediately, an officer picked up my mom up and said, "Excuse me, Ma'am! We're trying to arrest this man for shoplifting."

The officer, Lannie Claybar, with whom I went to high school, asked, "Isn't that Father Jim's mother?"

I'm looking around like, "Nope. No, it's really not. I don't know who that is…" And I kept walking!

But you see, that's not surprising for me when it comes to my mother. Why? I know and understand my mom. I knew that her heart was in the right place. I knew that she tried to reach out and help.

I think many people lose trust in the Lord precisely because they don't understand God. We have such unrealistic expectations of God. Some of us hold God to things He never promised us. God never promised us everything we want.

God promised us everything we need.

Everything we want is not necessary. Everything we need is. Many of us get caught up in the materialistic wants of our society. These particular wants, whether it's a car, a "perfect" family, the ultimate career, etc., can distract us from what we need: a personal, faith-based relationship with Jesus Christ. You have to trust.

God said, "You will join me on the cross of salvation." As Roman

Catholics, as Christians, we are going to have to endure this same cross. Every one of us is going to face and endure some form of crucifixion in life. Suffering is part of living in a broken world. I pray daily for my parishioners and the people in my life to be spared from sorrow. Still, I know some of them won't be, and they will need to pick up their crosses. It's a part of our walk in getting to know Jesus. We suffer with Him.

And guess what? We're going to have the choice. You can either run from it or run to it and embrace it. You can name it, claim it, and tame it, or you can fight it and allow it to cause tension.

In our personal lives, we must get to know people and understand them to know their hearts, to know what it is that they intend to do before it even happens.

It is the same with God.

I knew my mother attempted to save a man's life in good faith. This might be misguided, perhaps, in the passion of the moment, but behind her actions were the right reasons.

God has a plan for us all, and, to know our plan, we must first know God. One of the things we can truly ask ourselves on a daily basis is: "Do I know God well enough to know His calling, His invitation, for me?"

Several years ago, I received a call informing me of the death of my former sixth-grade Religion teacher, Sister Beatrice. She was 104-years-old. Hearing my gasp, the caller said, "You know Father, she was 104-years-old."

I responded, "Well, I thought she was 104 back in sixth grade!"

The wake was held in the MotherHouse Chapel. When I arrived, I happened to get behind two very elderly nuns. They talked to each other in loud voices. I guessed neither of them could hear very well.

As they approached Sr. Beatrice's casket, one sister turned to the other and said, "Is that Beatrice?"

The other replied, "I think so."

Then the other sister said, "Is she dead?"

To which the other sister answered, "I don't know, they don't tell us anything!"

I wonder how well we "listen in" when we ask the Holy Spirit to speak to us; to cleanse our ears, to hear God's voice and His word.

In Luke 10:38-42, we see where Martha is complaining to Jesus about Mary who is sitting at the feet of Jesus, listening to Him.

The Lord said to Martha's complaint, "Martha, Martha, you are anxious and worried about many things. There is need of only one thing; Mary has chosen the better part."

Now, we don't need to gang up on Martha. If we don't do any work, our prayers won't be put into action. However, we must see that prayer begins with listening to God. We must be willing to listen to God and then act upon what He is telling us. Then we can start the work.

S — Submit/Surrender

The "S" in T.R.U.S.T stands for submit, or surrender. If we want a deeper trust in the Lord, then we must be willing to "let go and let God."

Recently, I flew back from Rome on a beautiful aircraft, the 777, also known as the Triple 7. It's absolutely wonderful. If you haven't been on it, you should give it a try! They have a little TV in front of you that shows exactly where the plane is going. How fast. How high. What the temperature is outside. (I'm not sure why you need to know any of this, but, anyway, it's all right there.)

We flew nonstop from Rome to Chicago. As we made our final descent and were getting ready to land, the tires touched down. Then immediately, the little TV showed 100-, 200-, 300-feet, and I realize we were taking off again!

I'm screaming to the person sitting next to me (who I don't even know), "Oh my gosh! We're taking off again! Why isn't the pilot talking to us? Shouldn't he be sharing what's happening? Shouldn't he be telling us what's going on?"

The man remained calm and just turned to me and said, "Father, maybe the pilot is busy flying the plane."

I turned right back to him and said, "Well, now I know why I didn't talk to you the whole flight…"

But it's true. In that moment, I had no control over what happened.

As difficult as it was, I needed to let go. I needed to let God take control. Nothing more I could do in that moment to ensure my safety, and the safety of others, other than pray.

Well, I obviously survived. For whatever reason, which I do not know to this day, the pilot took back off, circled around, and landed again. For good that time.

All too often, we forget to pray and just let God take control. And we, for our own reasons, don't like that idea. We like to know exactly what is happening at every moment. Why is that? Why do we insist upon knowing what is going to happen? We must know because it gives us not only a sense of control but of ownership — a sense of authority.

This is difficult for many of us who believe that we are in charge. It's important for us to realize the difference between ownership and stewardship.

Ownership says, "Everything that I have is mine, and I can do with it what I please."

Stewardship says, "Everything we have is a gift from God, ultimately belongs to God, and is given freely back to God to use as He pleases."

It's that total submission, or surrender, that we find in stewardship.

God says to us over and over again, "I'm going to take care of you. I love you too much to let you go. I don't want you to worry about useless things, because I have already taken care of them. I am here and, I will never let you go!"

Take a moment as you read these words and look back at the struggles, the trials in your life. You are here and able to read these words at this very moment, because God is always with you. God will always be with you. God has already proven to you that He is going to take care of you. So, believe. Believe — trust and recognize God's presence in your life.

However, in order to surrender, in order to submit, we have to do something that is difficult for many of us. We have to obey. We must be willing to obey Him in all things. To be able to say, "I goofed. I did wrong."

Remember, it is the Ten Commandments, not the Ten Suggestions! When we do wrong, when we disobey, we have to repent through confession and move forward. I can't believe we don't have longer lines in our confessionals! What an amazing sacrament, a sacrament in which you can give and receive God's mercy and healing. The letting go, the dropping of the weight that threatens to crush us. Through confession, we can let go of our burdens and let God nail them to the cross.

So often I hear people share, "I don't need to confess my sins to a priest — I can go directly to God." And many people say, "I don't like confession" or "I don't believe that this sacrament is for me!"

Well, guess what? It's not about you! It's about something much greater. It's about God's grace! That ever-living, always-renewing grace of God that is exhibited, received, and fully given in the Sacrament of Confession.

As a member of a Universal Church, we are about more than ourselves, or our individual wants and needs. We are about something much, much more...

Community!

T — Try

How many of you reading this know the story of Peter walking on the water? Don't worry, I'm not going to know if you do or don't. But for those of you who don't, let's take a look at that story.

The disciples went to go fishing one day. They were in small boats on the Sea of Galilee when a huge storm rose up. Jesus, who didn't join them on the trip, appears, and is walking on the water toward them. The disciples are a bit surprised, to say the least, and no one says anything.

That is, except Peter.

We need to remember something very important. Peter suggested that he, himself, walk on water. Peter said, "Jesus, if it is really You, tell me to come to You across the water."

Jesus tells him, "Come on out, Peter."

What do you think all of the other apostles in the boat did at that moment? You know they probably laughed at his expense and criticized him. "Yeah, go on out there. You're the one who opened your mouth — just like you're always doing, Peter."

But Peter did it; he got out of the boat. Because at that moment, Peter possessed a deep trust. First of all, Peter had spent a lot of time with Jesus. And, as he spent time with Jesus, Peter developed a relationship with Jesus. They knew one another. Peter understood Jesus. And, in turn, Jesus understood Peter. Peter watched Jesus as He raised people from the dead. Peter saw Jesus heal people. He knew what Jesus could do. And Jesus, in turn, knew what Peter could do.

And after Peter opened his mouth, he must have known that walking on water is humanly impossible.

So, what happened?

He submitted to Jesus. He surrendered. And Peter stepped from the boat to walk on the water.

But then what happened after he took his first step?

Those of you who know the story are going to say, "But he didn't walk on the water. He sank." And you know what? He did. But here's the thing. He tried because he believed. He had faith. Peter knew that walking on water was humanly impossible, but he submitted to Christ's leading.

Then, his fear got the better of him.

This story of Peter, for some reason, reminds me of something my father used to always say to me during church when I was a boy. He'd say, "Jimmy, don't criticize those people up there unless you feel that you can do better, because they're trying."

All my sisters and brothers were asked to do was try. Trust as Peter trusted, and try. God takes our halting, stumbling efforts and transforms them into something beautiful. You see, God doesn't ask for perfection. He doesn't even ask that we get a "passing grade." He just asks us to step out of our little boats and join Him.

Jesus Touches Our Lives

Jesus challenges us to bring healing to a broken world. How do we do that? He calls us to seek justice and reach out to those who are poor. By "poor," he means the financially poor, the physically poor, the mentally poor, and the spiritually poor. If you think about it, that statement probably covers all of us in one way or another. Yet, Jesus also challenges us to reach out to those we think are untouchable; such as people in prison or someone dying of AIDS. True love, according to Our Lord, comes from loving those who might be completely different from us.

Winter in Massachusetts can be brutal. The cold is damp and driven by the wind. It feels like needles going through your bare skin, and it seems impossible to get warm most of the time.

During my college days in Boston, I got called into Symphony Hall. I waited for my subway car, shivering, along with a sea of people during rush hour. As the train came to a stop, I squeezed into the subway car by wedging myself between two people. (You have to be aggressive in large cities — no one is going to move to make space for you.)

As the doors shut, an odor filled the air: an odor that smelled like an unwashed body, onions, and a urinal in a bathroom. People put scarves around their noses, and I even heard a few people gag.

I looked through the crowd of people to see a disheveled homeless man. His gray beard, matted and full of dirt, came down to his chest. The poor man's watery red eyes suggested an addiction of some kind, most likely alcohol.

To my shame, I prayed, "Dear God, please don't send that man my way. Because God, we've discussed this. You constantly send these people to me, and I'm not ready for it. In Jesus' name, Amen.

Remember what I said about God answering prayers with a "No?"

As soon as I said, "Amen," the man looked at me and started walking. This man parted the crowd in that subway car like the Red Sea, and he looked straight at me.

As the car came to the next stop, which was Copley Square, he started reaching out to me and asked me a question. Intentionally, I turned my back to him. This man, covered in fecal matter, stained with urine, and full of open sores. I couldn't even face him.

As the car came to an abrupt stop, he slammed into a woman wearing a white mink coat, and he simply asked her, "Do you have a quarter?"

The woman gave him a dollar.

The doors opened to the subway. He stepped down, and immediately — within a millisecond — a voice came into my head: "James William Sichko — if that were my Son, you also denied Him."

Tears came flowing out of my eyes. I jumped off of the subway (remember, this all occurred within milliseconds) and looked everywhere, but the man had disappeared. I don't mean disappeared into the crowed. I mean he vanished into thin air.

No one can convince me this man wasn't an angel or maybe even Christ himself. And, I did a poor job of serving the people I considered to be the "least of these."

You see, in God's way of viewing things, the people we consider most important, God considers the least important. The powerful, the rich, the influential, are all laughed at by God. Don't believe me?

Read Psalm two. The Kingdom of God is for the weak and Jesus is the face of those people.

How well do you recognize that in your own life? Do you detest the lowest of the low? Are you good at recognizing what one preacher called "God's upside-down economy?" You must come to Him with nothing. You have to lay down your wealth, power, and influence if you want to get to know Him. God does everything upside-down in comparison to us.

Find the people in your life that you've normally ignored or despised. Who are they? For people on the right side of politics, it might be that liberal at work who voted for Obama twice. For the liberal, it might be that conservative who listens to Rush Limbaugh every day. What about the gay person everyone picks on at school? Or how about that bully who will stop at nothing to make your life miserable?

See, this is how challenging Jesus is to our lives. He wants us to see Him in everyone and treat everyone like we would treat Him.

No doubt, this is easier said than done.

Speeding

All of us have a secret weakness. Want to know mine? I drive fast. Really fast. NASCAR fast. As you can imagine, with my speaking schedule, I'm on the road a lot with plenty of opportunities to meet nice police officers from various states. You don't believe me? Here are some examples.

Wichita, Kansas — pulled over.

Hays, Kansas — pulled over.

Providence, Rhode Island — pulled over.

Interstate 55, Mississippi — pulled over.

Everywhere, Kentucky — pulled over (too many times to count).

I know; it's terrible. Believe me, the bishop lets me know every time he sees me. What can I say? The Lord is working on me to lighten my lead foot.

I went with a friend of mine, Father Armando, to a conference not too long ago. We drove along the Mountain Parkway, just outside out Lexington. I looked over to Father and said, "The speed limit is seventy around here, but I think I'm pushing eighty. I should probably slow down because it's not really safe. And, uh, my license is expired."

He looked at me. "You're not kidding, are you?"

I raised my hand. "Hey, I've been meaning to get to it. We'll be fine, there aren't many cops—"

Before I could complete the sentence, I looked in my rearview mirror. Sure enough, I saw not one, but two Kentucky State Troopers.

I said to my friend, "Father, there must have been an accident. Let's say a prayer."

Father Armando exclaimed, "The accident must be here, because they're right behind us!"

One trooper got out of his vehicle and came over to me. As I rolled down the window, he asked, "Father, do you realize why I pulled you over?"

I said, "No, not really."

Note to self: will need to confess this before Mass on Sunday.

The trooper shook his head. "Do you know how fast you were going?"

"Seventy-three?" I suggested.

All of a sudden, my brother priest, said, "Jim, you just told me you were going eighty!"

I just turned and stared at him. I'd ask forgiveness later for wanting to strangle him.

The trooper then said, "Okay, well I'm going to need to see your driver's license and your proof of insurance."

My helpful friend decides to chime in, "Don't look at the expiration date of the license — it's expired."

I confess to you, my brothers and sisters, that murder crossed my mind. I mean, here is my friend, my fellow priest, getting me into even more trouble with the police. What was his problem??

Then the Holy Spirit spoke to me.

Father Armando was right and I was wrong. My friend held me accountable and reminded me of my responsibility. I chose to drive fast, knowing the potential consequences, and with an expired license.

Chastened, I accepted my ticket and moved on down the road.

Our God handles us the same way. God forgives us for our

sinfulness. But, just because He is forgiving, doesn't mean He doesn't hold us accountable for our sins.

Sin isn't a very popular topic. We don't like to talk about it very much, but it's a must. Why? You can't get well until you admit you're sick and go to the doctor. I'm always amazed at the great lengths people will go to avoid admitting they've done wrong, hurt someone or just plain disobeyed God. The more we deny the problems of our heart, the further away we get from Christ.

The sad thing is that we do it to ourselves, because we think if we admit sin, God will strike us down. It's the opposite. God wants us to come to Him with our sin so He can make us clean. This is what confession is all about, getting clean, getting a fresh start and God pressing the do-over button. We don't realize that God's grace to the truly repentant is never-ending. If we did, I think I'd be busy doing confessions before Mass. I'd like that problem.

Here is another thing you need to know. I'm a sinner too. I go to confession. There are sin burdens on my own heart that I need to lie down. I confess to a fellow priest who absolves me. You know what? I can't tell you how free I feel afterward.

And yes, I even confess when I break the law by speeding.

Third-Graders

I love visiting the kids at our parish elementary school. They challenge me every time I talk to them through their innocence and their wisdom. Seems like an odd combination, but it's been my experience the more innocent among us are usually the most wise. The rest of us are too weighed down with our perceived "real-life" problems to see the obvious. I think this is why Jesus told us that no one comes to Him unless they have the faith of a child.

As I entered the kindergarten class, the children sat on a rug while the teacher taught them about colors. They invited me to participate and I asked the kids, "Can you tell me what color apples are?"

Hands shot to the sky. One thing I've learned is that you never want to call on the first person who raises their hand. In this situation, a little boy named David bounced up and down to get my attention. Usually, the first kid to raise their hand says something completely not related to the topic. The observation goes something like this: "This one time, I saw a squirrel run and stare at me. Then he talked to me. It was cool."

So, to avoid that conversation, I called on a little girl who answered, "Apples are red."

I said, "Yes, that's true, that's correct. Apples are red."

Another boy answered and said, "Apples are green."

"That's also correct."

Another girl raised her hand and answered, "Sometimes apples are yellow."

I agreed with the girl, but, again, little David waved his hand, insisting to be recognized. I sighed and said, "Alright, David. What color are apples?"

He said, "Father, apples are white!"

All the little kids giggled.

"Uh, David, I don't believe I've ever seen a white apple." I didn't want to make the kid feel stupid in front of his friends, so I adopted my "fake" thoughtful look.

Before I could move on, David stood up and said, "Father, haven't you ever bitten an apple before? It's white on the inside."

Everyone got quiet, and I said, "David, you're right. Apples are white. We all just need to look a little deeper."

Throughout all of life, we quickly learn that what's on the outside is not necessarily what lies deep within. We, as Catholics, as Christians, are called to cultivate that which lies deep inside every one of us — our souls.

In this situation, it was through the teaching of a child that I was once again reminded to look beyond the outward appearance, the physical handicaps, the annoying behavior, and to realize that what lies deep within each human is a heart. We must seek a heart that seeks the love of Christ through another. A heart, in which is instilled with, and created through, the great love God has for each of our lives.

C.S. Lewis wrote a great book called *The Last Battle*. It's the final book in his fantastic *Chronicles of Narnia* series. I don't want to give too much away, but the main characters all go to what amounts to heaven in the land of Narnia.

Aslan, Lewis's stand in for Christ in the books, encourages everyone to come "further up, further in." The idea is for us to press toward the heart of Narnia, heaven itself, where Aslan resides.

That is what God want us to do. He wants us to press "further up, further in" to Him. He wants us to step through each "door," and reveal a wider world of Himself. Let me tell you, that world is endless, each part of Him bigger than the last.

Some people ask what we will be doing during eternity in heaven. My answer?

The same thing we do here. We'll be getting to know Him.

The Mouse Story

A mouse looked through a crack in the wall
to see the farmer and his wife opening a package.
"What food might this contain?" The mouse wondered.
He was devastated to discover it was a mousetrap.
Retreating to the farmyard,
the mouse proclaimed a warning:
"There is a mousetrap in the house!
There is a mousetrap in the house!"

The chicken clucked and scratched,
raised her head, and said, "Mr. Mouse,
I can tell this is of grave concern to you,
but it is of no consequence to me.
I cannot be bothered by it."

The mouse turned to the pig and told him,
"There is a mousetrap in the house!
There is a mousetrap in the house!"

The pig sympathized, but said,
"I am so very sorry, Mr. Mouse,
but there is nothing I can do about it but pray.
Be assured, you are in my prayers."

The mouse turned to the cow and said,
"There is a mousetrap in the house!
There is a mousetrap in the house!"

The cow said, "Wow, Mr. Mouse. I'm sorry for you,
but it's no skin off my nose."

So, the mouse returned to the house,
with his head down and dejected,
to face the farmer's mousetrap alone...

That very night,
a sound was heard throughout the house
— the sound of a mousetrap catching its prey.

The farmer's wife rushed to see what was caught.
In the darkness, she did not see it.
It was a venomous snake
whose tail was caught in the trap.

The snake bit the farmer's wife.
The farmer rushed her to the hospital.

When she returned home, she still had a fever.
Everyone knows how you treat a fever —
with fresh chicken soup.
So the farmer took his hatchet to the farmyard
for the soup's main ingredient.

But his wife's sickness continued.
Friends and neighbors
came to sit with her
around the clock.
To feed them,

the farmer butchered the pig.
But, alas,
the farmer's wife did not get well...
she died.

So many people came for her funeral
that the farmer had the cow slaughtered
to provide enough meat for everyone
at the funeral luncheon.

And the mouse looked upon it all
from his crack in the wall
with great sadness.

So, the next time you hear that
someone is facing a problem
and you think it doesn't concern you,
remember —

When one of us is threatened, we are all at risk.
We are all involved in the journey called "Life."
We must keep an eye out for one another
and make an extra effort
to encourage one another.

And let them know how important they are.
Each one is a vital threat,
In another person's tapestry.
Our lives are woven together.
For a reason.

Random Acts
of Kindness

Recently, while traveling, I gassed up my rental car at the city's local BP station. On the opposite side of the pump, an old, used, worn-out truck (what we would describe in Kentucky as a "farm truck"), pulled up to get some gas.

Inside, I saw an older, white-haired gentleman and a kid I assumed must be his grandchild. I watched as they searched for loose change by looking through the consoles and the ashtray.

I know people might think I'm crazy, but God speaks to me (as He does to everyone, if they listen). I'm confident of it.

In this case, His whispering voice said, Pay for their gas.

And, while I'm convinced God speaks to me, I also fight him a lot. This time, the following thoughts ran through me.

Who do I think I am? What would they say? I'm a complete stranger. What if I offend them?

The Holy Spirit answered (I'm paraphrasing just a bit), poked me hard in the spiritual ribs, and said, "Get going, my son." The Advocate loves us enough to give us a good swift kick when we need it. In this case, I needed the reminder of practicing what I preached: walk the walk, etc., and so on.

I leaned across the fuel bay, stuck my BP card in the credit-card reader and paid for their gas.

The older gentleman, as I expected, asked, "What are you doing?"

I said, "I'm purchasing your gas today!"

"Do I know you?"

I replied, "You do now!"

"What's your name?"

I smiled. "I'm Mr. BP and I'm traveling around the city giving away free gas."

The man grinned ear to ear at this and told his grandson, "Boy, did you hear that? Mr. BP bought our gas today! When we get home, you are going to have a great story to share with your momma!"

He made his grandson get out of the truck, and they thanked me together. Then he said to the child, "Never forget this moment and what is being done for us, because we, in turn, someday, must do the same for others!"

I didn't tell this story so you'd think I'm a swell guy. I think I've demonstrated my capacity to sin and make mistakes. Instead, I'm using it to show how God speaks to us so that we can help others.

A lot of people can't quote all of the Ten Commandments. God knows we're forgetful people, so Jesus summed up His law in two simple statements: Love the Lord your God with all your heart and with all your soul and with all your mind. And love your neighbor as yourself.

———

Many people come up to me and ask what great thing they can do for the faith. Very often, they're leaders in the church looking to make some grand gesture. I usually pat them on the arm and say, "Help us scrub floors. Help us serve the older folks. Help us teach the children. Help us find the unspoken needs in our parish."

I say these things so leaders can understand what Jesus meant when he commanded the apostles to love one another.

During the Last Supper, Jesus took off his garments and washed the disciples' feet. Now, in our modern time, we don't understand the significance of this gesture. In those days, people walked with open-toed sandals or no footwear at all. Animals used the road (take a guess what they did on it), people would throw their household waste in the streets, and people would walk through all this slop.

So, when you washed someone's feet back then, it could be a pretty revolting task. Jesus did it for his disciples and commanded them to do likewise. His point? That simple, small things show how much of a leader you can be through being a servant.

Trusting the voice of the Holy Spirit and recognizing that voice will call all of us to practice our faith to the maximum. If we are going to be people who trust, if we are going to be people who have faith, then we are going to have to be people who take risks — who are challenged to go outside of our comfort zone and reach within ourselves to reach out to others.

So often we allow our fears to rob us of the opportunity to do good for others. We like being comfortable and are afraid to risk stepping outside of our own comfort zones. We are afraid to risk following the Spirit as the Holy Spirit leads us to do the work of the Lord — feeding the sick, helping the outcast, being a friend to the marginalized, smiling at the stranger, and recognizing Christ in the person who is most different from us.

When I am faced with such a situation, I never want to ask the question, "If I stop to help this man, what will happen to me?" Instead, I must turn this question around and ask, "If I do not stop to help this man, what will happen to him?"

What did I learn from the gas station experience?

First, I learned that TRUST in the Holy Spirit means recognizing that voice, that call, and knowing, even as difficult as it may be, that I must follow through wherever the Holy Spirit leads me. Second, from this small, random act of kindness, came an opportunity for another to evangelize and share the Good News.

"As you did it to one of the least of these, you did it to me."

So, I didn't just serve these lovely people; I served Christ Himself.

It is a sad day when it takes a tragedy to awaken the need of reaching out, in kindness, to a total stranger. It is my own personal belief that we need to begin asking ourselves, "Why aren't we doing this regularly?"

The problem is not that we aren't a generous people. The problem lies in being people who are not able to "receive" gifts that are given to us. Often times, I find that people are not open in receiving. Acts of kindness, believe it or not, can be uncomfortable for both the giver and the receiver.

As you might guess, 8:30 Sunday morning Mass is a rough go for me. Afterward, I require a trip to the Starbucks drive-thru where I order the "Father Jim Special," which consists of three shots of espresso in a venti cup filled with whipped cream. (Don't ask!)

It is my tradition to always pay for the car behind me, regardless of their order or cost. As I reach out the window with my new cell phone, which contains my Starbucks card app to pay for the purchases, the barista drops my phone, cracking the screen.

"Oh Father, I'm so sorry. Just back up your car and see if you can reach it."

You probably figure where this is going.

I put the car in reverse, back up, and smash my phone. I just stared at it, reflecting how just days ago, I went to the same Starbucks, paid for the car behind me and the barista dropped that phone. The one I'm staring at happened to be the replacement.

Immediately, I thought to myself, No more Starbucks and no more random acts of kindness for those behind me!

I know it makes no sense to blame an act of kindness for my misfortune. But people often lash out unfairly and blame others when they're upset. Some may think it reasonable to stop giving, stand on the sidelines and not get involved. But we must always remember the work of Jesus; the life of a person of faith involves getting out of our comfort zone and taking a risk. In every situation of our lives, we have the opportunity, the choice to always show mercy to another. Even if it means we break dozens of phones, God calls us to love our neighbor.

Whenever we are faced with a desire to assist, we must listen to the Holy Spirit and allow the Divine to overpower our own human frailties, that is when God's grace becomes sufficient and manifests into reality. The power of the Advocate can consume our doubts with His fire and make us brave.

Lies

Honesty is a golden key to living. Once you start being dishonest, you start being responsible for your lies. Those lies require maintenance. They require care. And soon, they devour all of your attention. You're going to have to be accountable for those lies. And I'm here to tell you something. They'll come back to haunt you.

I taught at a very prestigious Catholic high school as a priest. I taught these wonderful senior students. I required only one major rule to be adhered to in my classroom, aside from respecting and knowing your boundaries: One particular Monday in March you could not be absent.

On that day, I gave their final exam. It couldn't be missed. The only excusable absence I gave would be if I read my student's name in the obituaries, or the name of one of their parents. And even then, I would have wanted a written note from the funeral director.

Mind you, I reminded the students of this rule on the first, second, third, fourth, and fifth day that I taught them in the classroom. I placed the information in every syllabus I gave them. No one could plead ignorance.

Lo and behold, the big day of the exam arrived, and two of my top pupils turned up a "no show." I immediately phoned the funeral home. No bodies. I called the hospitals and even the police stations. Nothing.

The next day, Tuesday morning, the two missing students entered my classroom and said, "Did you know we weren't in class yesterday?"

I looked up from my grading work and calmly replied, "Really? No, I hadn't noticed."

They responded almost in unison, "Well, we weren't."

I sat back in my chair. "And, why is that, when you know I accept no excuses for missing the exam."

As they scrambled for the right words, I tried not to laugh or cry. I felt like doing both.

"Well, here's the reason, Father Jim. We went to visit a college. It was the University of Notre Dame. Did you know, Father, that Notre Dame is a Catholic college?"

I nodded my head for them to continue.

They said, "Oh yeah, Father. Big-time Catholic school. And, while we were there, we went to church at the Basilica located on campus. After we got out of Mass, we went to our car, and one of our tires was flat. We thought to ourselves, Father Jim wouldn't want us to drive home late at night, because, by the time we found someone to change the tire, it was already dark. So, after weighing the options, we thought you would want us to come back safe and, if need be, miss the exam..."

I cut them off and said, "You know what? You are exactly right. You can take the test tomorrow morning."

They looked at each other in almost comic disbelief.

They lavished me with praise, "What? No way! Father, you're the coolest! Don't care what anyone in this school says about you. You rock! You're the best!"

So, when the two pupils arrived the next morning, I put one in Mrs. Wyatt's classroom across the hall, and I put the other in Mrs. Hays's room, right next door. I gave each of the students their exam, which was comprised of two pieces of paper, with one question on each page.

Question 1 – What is your name?
Question 2 – Which tire was flat?
Exactly.
One student answered, "Front left."
The other answered, "Front right."
They had lied!
Case closed. I failed both of those students. And having failed my class, both students didn't graduate, because religion represented a large percentage of the overall grade point average. Such a consequence may seem harsh. But they made a terrible choice to skip the test and then lie to me on top of it.

What I did was hold them accountable and responsible for their actions. There is nothing wrong with holding people accountable for the choices that they freely make.

These same students call me now, and can you guess what they say to me?

"Thank you."

Believe it or not, they thank me for taking a difficult stance and providing the boundaries they needed, and for which they longed.

There is a special responsibility placed upon those of you reading these words who are parents. You're responsible to be a parent first to your child — not a friend. Friendship will develop as maturity develops. There is nothing wrong with discipline in a correct, caring, and loving way.

To the children who might read this book, I'll offer this advice: you are called to use your parents as a valuable resource. You're called to learn from your mistakes and use your parents to help you, to challenge you, to sustain you, and to move you forward in life.

I remember the first and only time that I talked back to my mother. As an eight-year-old, I started to feel my independence. I was lying on the floor watching TV. We had just finished eating dinner, and my father sat on the couch.

My mother called out from the kitchen, "Jimmy, come and clean off the dining room table, please."

I yelled out, "No!"

The last thing I remember is my father picking me up by the ear, taking me into the bathroom, and feeding me a bar of Irish Spring soap.

I can assure you that my father didn't abuse me. Nor did I need to seek counseling for "soap issues." My father, who loved me very much, taught me a valuable lesson about respecting and obeying one of the commandments of Jesus. Honor your father and your mother.

Have I ever talked back to my mother since? Nope. Do I have convulsions when I go to the supermarket and pass bars of Irish Spring soap? You bet.

Remember, we're all in this relationship together, teaching, learning, and growing. Within our church, there is a similar community — a family of its own. And we are all part of the greater community and family of God.

Listen With Your Heart

I love New York City — the sounds, the sirens, the hustle and bustle! It's where I find the greatest "peace" within me. Recently, while walking down Madison Avenue with a good friend of mine, I commented to him, "Listen to the birds chirp!"

He responded, "Excuse me?"

So I repeated myself. "Listen to the birds chirp!"

He looked at me quizzically and said, "I think you need a sabbatical. The only things I hear are sirens, buses, people yelling, and cabs honking their horns!"

Immediately, I reached into my pocket, grabbed a handful of loose coins, and threw them up in the air. When they hit the sidewalk, people came from everywhere, trying to find and pick up the loose coins strewn about.

People hear what they want to hear! If you open your Bible sometime, read Matthew 28:16-30. There is a passage there that is referred to as "The Great Commission."

Let me set the scene for you. Jesus rose from the dead. During Jesus' ministry, His disciples experienced Him raising people from the dead, healing people who were sick, and even casting out demons from individuals who were possessed.

Most importantly, the disciples watched Jesus be crucified; they witnessed his painful and horrific death. And now, through this passage, we find that Jesus has returned to them, alive again, raised by God himself. But even so, the Scripture writer makes it clear that some of the disciples still doubted that this was Jesus.

They struggled to believe. They were not ready to put their full faith and trust in Him. If we are really honest with ourselves, this is no different than many of us who are reading this text. We know that Jesus died for us, that Jesus rose for us, and that He lives forever, but, even so, we resist putting our lives into His hands or following where He leads.

But, I am here to tell you, as a priest, preacher, teacher, and Christian, Jesus was there that day. He was real, He was raised from the dead, and He is alive forever. It is no different for us today, regardless of where we are on our journeys in life. Jesus is real, Jesus is alive, and Jesus is present with us this very moment.

Read the passage from Matthew again, and really listen to what Jesus says. Before He tells His disciples what to do, He tells them more about who He is. "All authority has been given to me in heaven and on earth."

And then, He exercises this unlimited authority by giving His disciples — and, in essence, each of us — a mission, a job, an assignment. Actually, it is the greatest mission ever set forth in history. "Go, therefore, and obey everything I have commanded you. Go and make disciples of all the nations — everybody, the whole earth." Do not leave any corner untouched, any stone unturned. It is an awesome assignment, and it requires faith.

Recently, I took a flight, and I sat in my usual spot, the emergency exit window. The plane began its initial descent into this particular airport. All of a sudden, something happened that I have always heard of but had never experienced as an avid traveler. We hit what they call "clear air turbulence." Our plane dropped 3,000 feet in about five seconds. I remember immediately grabbing onto whatever I could, and that happened to be the hair of the woman sitting directly in front of me. I screamed at the top of my lungs.

After the plane regained its altitude, I felt an individual staring at me. I turned to my right, and across the aisle, a young business executive, dressed in a suit, looked directly at me.

In the hush of the moment, the gentleman, whom I do not know and have not seen since, immediately blurted out, "Not good PR, Father! As the plane was dropping, we were looking to you for faith! We were looking to you that all would be well. We were looking to you for faith in Jesus Christ! And, what did we find? We found you screaming and pulling the hair of my wife, sitting in front of you!"

I immediately looked back at him and said, "Are you Catholic?"

He responded, "No!"

I whispered to myself, "Thank God."

Who are we? And what do we profess to be? Being a Christian, being a Catholic, is not a one-day-a-week job. It is a lifetime assignment in which we continually challenge ourselves by what we profess and how we live.

Who are people of faith in your life? Who are the real people, whom you know personally, who are examples of Jesus and His church for you? Learn from them, grow with them, and share about them.

Boxing and Brothers

Both of my brothers graduated from the US Naval Academy in Annapolis, Maryland. One of the training requirements at the Academy is to take up a sport, and one of my brothers took up the sweet science of boxing. He loved every minute of it and tried to convince me to go with him to matches.

Now, think about it. I'm a priest, and a classically-trained singer. I'm not exactly the first person to show up at an event where men beat each other to a bloody pulp. Still, I love my brothers and we enjoy hanging out with other. When they invited me to attend a boxing match in Vegas for a holiday get away, I decided to go.

Las Vegas is always an interesting study of contrasts. On one hand, there are the magic shows, amusements parks and the family side of one of the world's greatest party towns. Then, there is the dark side of Gamblers Anonymous, prostitution, the strip clubs, and people's lives being ruined. The city is one big living contrast.

So, why would a priest of God be in this town at all? Well, first, I love spending time with my brothers. Second, I believe Jesus would be there, among the gamblers, the boxers, the prostitutes, and the shady types. Too often people think church is for good people. Let me tell you, it's not. The church is a place for sinners to be healed.

To me, the church must stop presenting itself as "holier than thou" and get in the muck. This is why I love Pope Francis and the attitude he is bringing to the Catholic Church. He wants us to be with sinners like ourselves, tell them about Jesus and the love of His church.

Those types of thoughts drove me to wear my clericals to the boxing match. I don't wear them to make people uncomfortable. Rather, I like to remind people that God is everywhere with them. Not because I'm God (yikes, what a scary thought!), but because the clericals represent the church who represents God. I like people to know He loves them and is always looking out for them.

So, picture me walking with my brothers to our ringside seats. Everyone whispered as I sat down. I couldn't hear exactly what they said, but it probably went something like, "Man, how did Father score those seats? Does he know the Pope or something?"

As we sat down before the match, we watched the two legendary fighters make their way to the ring. Thousands of people stood on their feet and roared their approval. Music played so loudly that it hurt my ears. Both boxers — Oscar De La Hoya and Floyd Mayweather — entered the ring, shadowboxing, alone with their thoughts even in a sea of people.

De La Hoya entered the ring, raised his arms, and began to dance. He saw my collar and caught my eyes. Everyone watched as he made his way over to me and leaned over the ropes. I glanced up at the Jumbotron to see me and the legendary boxer in large, bright colors across the large-screen display.

The fighter marked himself with the Sign of the Cross through his tethered boxing gloves, kissed his hands, and saluted me. I gave him a little wave, said a blessing, and he moved on to his corner. The crowd roared with delight.

My brother leaned over to me and asked, "Jimmy, will that help him win the match?"

I gave him half a smile, "Sure . . . if he knows how to box!"

Everything in life, whether religious or not, runs by certain ground rules.

First, as shared many times throughout this book, we must be people of faith who trust and are not afraid to risk. Risk requires us to go outside of our comfort zones.

Don't think you've got a comfort zone? Sure you do. Your personal zone might be any number of things, from your home and family to hiding some sort of addiction. Comfort zones are not always a good or positive force. They can hold you back from where God wants you to be. Good is no longer good if it stops us from listening to the Holy Spirit. You see, anything good can be twisted into bad through the sinfulness of the heart.

So, how does the Holy Spirit knock us out of own little worlds? He challenges us to not only hang out with people like us, but to seek out those who are different from us. The Gospels are full of stories of Jesus crossing lines, kicking cultural taboos, and going over any obstacle to reach "untouchable" people.

My parishioners and people who hear me at conferences get the same reminder: "How you treat others is how you treat Jesus."

In the Gospels, when Jesus talks about the Final Judgment in Matthew 24-25, He talks about the people who make it into His Kingdom. Who makes it? The people who feed the prisoner, love the loveless, welcome the stranger, and entertain angels without so much of a thought other than, "Jesus would be this way; so should I." This is the risk we take up when we agree to follow Jesus.

So, when we pray, it involves an element of risk. We risk God changing us and making us want different things. He reserves the right to challenge our zones and bring us into a new understanding. You must remember, to paraphrase C.S. Lewis, that He is not a "tame" God, nor is He a personal "house" idol under your control.

Also, remember, prayer and action must go together. God requires it because He blessed you by letting you participate in His answer. When we are praying to move those mountains spoken of in Matthew 17:20, we must remember to bring a shovel with us. People say there are two kinds of faith — a blue-denim variety and a rocking-chair one. With the former, we say we are willing to use the shovel to help get the job done. The latter says we expect God to do all of the heavy lifting for us. The ideal, then, is to pray as though everything depends on God, and work as though everything depends on you.

I know this next idea is a shocker, but God doesn't give you everything you might want. Thank God He doesn't. If I received eighty-percent of the things I thought I desperately wanted, I'd be in serious trouble. God knows better than we do. Plus, we must also remember other people might be involved in what we want. What if what you pray for is not good for them? That isn't to say God doesn't always answer prayers. He does, but as it's often been pointed out, His answer is sometimes, "No."

Saint Teresa of Avila said more tears are shed over answered prayers than over unanswered prayers. This may or not be true, but it illustrates a good point. God often allows us to have our way so we can learn a sharp lesson; our wants are often the worst thing for us. What we need is to pray, full of trust, that Our Father will take our prayers and make them right. "Let His will be done."

Prayer needs to be honest. Mark Twain nailed it when he wrote in *Huckleberry Finn,* "But deep down in me I knowed it was a lie, and He knowed it. You can't pray a lie—I found that out."

Too many times, I find myself and parishioners trying to pray in ways we think God would want us to pray. God doesn't want us to do that, because He already knows our hearts. What He wants is for us to lay out our real thoughts, the real "bottom of our hearts," so that He can transform us.

Side note: The Bible is one of the most honest books in the world. It presents human beings as we are, with all of our problems, hang-ups, and ugliness. So, if God knows how we are in His book, do you think you can hide from Him when you kneel in prayer? Of course not. Stop hiding, bring it all out and let Him fix it. Leave out the qualifying words such as, "If you do this, then I'll do that." Maybe you will, maybe you won't. God knows in either case.

Finally, as we should do with everything in life, our challenge when we pray should be to persevere in that prayer. Never, ever give up. We must always believe in what we pray, even in the darkest moments. God will never abandon us. All of us, at one time or another in our lives, feel abandoned, alone, or even lost. But, God was with us then, God is with us now, and God will always be with us. Why? Because we are His own. We are part of Him. We are His creation, whom He loves, respects, and, yes, even in our own sinfulness, He admires that which He made.

Waking Up for Pope John Paul II

One of the great dreams for any priest is to concelebrate with the Holy Father. Through some friends, I obtained this amazing privilege while Pope John Paul II remained with us. (The great thing about him was how he offered this privilege to many priests around the world.) Even more, we presided over the Mass in his private chapel, a beautiful section of the papal apartments.

As you can expect, I couldn't sit still on my flight to Rome. I kept pinching myself, finding it hard to believe I get to meet the pope.

I remember arriving in Rome in the afternoon. By the time I got to the North American College, right near the Vatican walls, I felt like dropping on the spot. The receptionist informed me that the Vatican called reconfirming my participation in Holy Father's morning Mass. They told me to be at the Bronze Doors by 6 a.m.

Even though I was tired, I couldn't shut my eyes to rest. I called my mom. I paced my room.

Sometime early in the morning, I heard helicopter blades just outside my room. I thought, Wow that must be the Pope arriving for morning Mass. You better get up and get ready. This is a graced filled day.

I shook myself awake but found myself confused. First, I looked at my watch and it said something like 10 o'clock. But how could that be right? I had to be at the Bronze Doors at 6 a.m. Maybe it was ten at night? However, I felt as if I had slept longer than that.

I opened up the "wooden shutter" in my room and glanced out the window. People walked the streets, and the sun was high in the sky.

As you can imagine, a wave of panic hit me like a truck. I ran out into the hall in my boxer shorts, trying to communicate with someone in English.

"What time is it?"

"Do you know what time it is?!"

I kept running back and forth inside the room and outside the room. I didn't know what to do, and the feeling was awful.

How could I have overslept and missed the opportunity to meet His Holiness? What would I tell my mother and friends back home?

"It was like a dream?"

I did oversleep. The jet lag did me in and I felt terrible.

Thankfully, I called around and they gave me a new opportunity. I set four alarms, all at different times. I still didn't go to sleep, because I didn't want to commit another grave faux pas.

Finally, the hour came, and I got to the Bronze Doors in time. They escorted me to a large marble staircase and then placed me in an elevator. When the doors opened, I found myself in the papal apartments. I sat with ten other Americans, priests and sisters, behind the Holy Father as he prayed. It's sort of amazing, the holy and human things you notice in this sort of situation. First, I couldn't help but notice his large ears. Then, kicking myself, I noticed how he prayed. He groaned as he lifted the weight of the world up to God.

After Mass, we all spread throughout his library. The Holy Father came to us individually and spoke to each one of us in our native tongue.

When Pope John Paul got to me, his secretary Monsignor Stanislaw Dziwisz (now Cardinal Dziwisz) introduced us. As I knelt down to kiss the pope's ring, he picked me up and said in his Polish accent, "It is good to see you awake." Then he smiled with a twinkle in his eye. We laughed, and I thanked him for the opportunity. I asked him to pray for me, my family, especially my mother and vocation. He gave me a rosary and then handed me another one while saying, "This is for your lovely mother."

As I recall this story, I am reminded of just three years ago, exactly around the anniversary date of my meeting His Holiness, my mother became suddenly, critically ill.

She and my sister decided to take their yearly visit to my house in Kentucky. Usually, they stay only five days. Even though I beg my mom to stay longer, she always says, "Jimmy, we're going home."

This time, however, something different happened. She said, much to our surprise, "Let's just stay another day."

When she woke up that next morning, she took a few steps out of bed and collapsed in a heap. I called 911, and then I called the bishop to pray for her.

We rushed her to the hospital. They diagnosed her with acute pancreatitis that soon sent her into acute respiratory syndrome and her kidneys began to fail. On top of all that, she turned septic. The doctors told us we needed to say our goodbyes, call funeral homes in both states, and notify family members.

Sitting in the parking lot of the hospital on the day I expected my mother to die, I remember facing the decision to install a tracheostomy tube and take her off the ventilator. As I prayed, I remembered this was the anniversary of meeting the Holy Father. I also remembered asking Pope John Paul to intercede on my mother's behalf, to whisper a prayer to God's ear and get my mother well.

I went up to the ICU unit at St. Joseph's Hospital East. A flurry of activity near ICU caught my attention.

Immediately, one of the nurses turned to me and said, "I think your mom is going to fly today!"

I wasn't sure what that meant, and my sister and I just looked at one another.

Then, my mother's doctor (as well as one of my parishioners), Dr. Kent Kessler, came out and informed us that our mother was being taken off the ventilator. She began to breathe on her own.

One of the doctors overseeing my mother's case said, "There is no doubt, this was a true miracle, Father..."

Later this year, Pope John Paul II will be made a saint of the Roman Catholic Church in a canonization ceremony. If there had ever been any question about miracles attributed to his intercession, I would have submitted this story.

Things Happen
for a Reason

On Sunday mornings, I have two Masses at which I normally preside: 8:30 a.m. (need coffee) and 11 a.m. The 8:30 a.m. crowd is much more "reserved" and quiet in nature, whereas the 11 a.m. crowd is livelier and more expressive. If you remember, my usual practice after the 8:30 a.m. Mass is a drive to the local Starbucks to get the "Father Jim Special." You should try it sometime if you're ever in Richmond, Kentucky.

On a certain Sunday morning, I drove to church so I could celebrate the 8:30 Mass, and I missed the usual exit for church. My thoughts were everywhere but getting off at the right exit. I decided to take the next exit and make my coffee run a bit earlier. I laughed at the thought of my 8:30 a.m. parishioners getting, "Turbo Father Jim."

As I departed from Starbucks with coffee in hand, I saw one of my parishioners, and I honked my horn. He stared at me with a "deer in headlights" look, and I wondered what could be wrong so early in the morning.

I rolled down my window and said, "Hey, what's going on, are you okay?"

He started to cry and said, "Father, I've made a huge mistake in my marriage. I'm so glad you're here. God sent you, I know."

We talked for a few moments, and he agreed to call me later in the day.

I'm often struck by how God breaks up routines to make things happen. Sometimes, it can be something as simple as a missed exit or a dead battery. He uses these little events to steer us to help others who are in serious trouble. And, if you think about it, God's probably done the same for you in your own life.

Why does He do it? I think it's because so often in life we're tempted to think God has abandoned us. We feel alone, tried, and isolated. When we do, I believe the Devil likes to take advantage of us at those times. He uses our sorrow, sadness, and feelings of being anxious for the future.

Stephen King once wrote that he's built his career on imagining "the worst that can possibly happen to people." He is a great writer because he knows how people function. We worry about the worst happening to us. We dread the phone call in the middle of the night. We get a knot in our stomach over the possibility of things like a letter from the bank saying our home is being foreclosed on, a child telling us he or she is a drug addict, or the spouse we love asking for a divorce.

The future is clouded and impossible for us to see. Jesus knows this because He talked about it in His famous Sermon on the Mount. He tells us that we shouldn't bother about tomorrow because it belongs to God. Concentrate on today, what is in front of you, and deal with those issues. Jesus also goes on to tell us that we can't add to our lives because we worry about it. Just the opposite. Medical science tells us that stress is probably the number-one killer through heart attacks, strokes, and various other diseases.

Stephen King, in the same discussion, talks about how the worst rarely happens, and it's for that reason he believes in God. He's hit on an important theological truth. God controls the world, has everything in His hands, and gives us the peace of Christ. When things are terrible, awful, and horrible, we must remember that God's mercy is with us, the Holy Spirit comforts us, and that Jesus suffered, too.

It's the last thing that gives me comfort during troubled time: Jesus, the son of God, suffers as we suffer.

When we feel forgotten, we need to remember Christ's words — his gift of peace, of an Advocate, of a guide who will look for us when we are lost, who will console us when we're filled with despair, and who will be there when we feel alone or abandoned.

"Do not let your hearts be troubled or afraid."

Be assured of this beautiful and amazing fact: we are not alone. No matter how thick the jungle or how dark the skies — God will find us. No matter how worried we might be — God will find us. In our troubled times. In our pain. In our uncertainty. In our fear. In our financial turmoil, relationship issues, depression, anxiety, and hurt — He will find us.

We are never, ever, forgotten or abandoned. All one has to do is open up the Scriptures and see the many reassurances that God gives us, that He isn't going to leave us.

"So do not fear for I am with you" (Isaiah 41:10). "Be strong and courageous. Do not be afraid or terrified because of them, for the Lord your God goes with you; He will never leave you or forsake you" (Deuteronomy 31:6).

We may leave God, but God will never leave us. No matter how bleak the situation, no matter how empty the feeling, God will never leave you or desert you. His promises are true. His Word is above all! We can move forward because He goes before us. And if God is for us, who can be against us? There is no one, no living creature like Him, and He will not allow His Word to return to Him empty.

Moving On

This past week, I greeted individuals at the entrance of our church who were attending the funeral of a longtime parishioner. A woman came up to me, introduced herself and then asked, "Who are you?"

"Oh, I'm Father Jim, the priest for this parish."

She gave me a funny look and said, "I'm a longtime parishioner here."

I'll be the first to admit I'm not the greatest with names. I'm well aware of faces, but my memory seems to fail me when it comes to specifics. I knew it could be possible I'd forgotten this woman's name because of my poor name skills.

Still, the fact that she didn't know who I was made me raise my eyebrows, considering I'd been the priest at this parish for the past nine years.

As she talked about being involved in the community, I interrupted her, "Now, are you sure it's this St. Mark?"

She gave me a look of irritation and said, "Yes, of course. I know Father Poole very well."

I felt this conversation entering *The Twilight Zone* as I said, "Well, Ma'am, Father Poole is now with Our Father in heaven. He died many years before I got here."

The poor woman looked at me in confusion, "Well, no one tells me anything!"

I hid my laughter but reflected on her words as I thought about a man I ran into at a restaurant near the church. Someone pointed out this man stopped coming to Mass, and I wanted to seek him out.

"Hey, we miss you at church. I'd really like to see you come back. Is there anything I can do?"

The man looked down and wouldn't look me in the eyes.

"Well, Father, I've done a lot of bad things recently. If I came to church, it would make me the worst hypocrite in the world."

I laughed and said, "There's always room for one more, my friend."

He glanced up at me, chuckled and said, "Okay, I'll be there on Sunday."

Both of these stories tell us about why we need to go to church. Just to be clear, sitting your butt down in the pew every Sunday doesn't make you holy. The very act of just being in the building isn't enough. Instead, it depends on knowing the living Jesus Christ, and knowing that the choice to follow him is vital. Everyone is responsible for their own faith in the end and our decisions do matter. Our choice is either the "smoking" (hell) or "non-smoking" (heaven) section. You can't lay the ultimate blame on other people for your loss of faith. Christ calls you as a person to decide whether you'll embrace Him.

The Holy Spirit calls and enables us to imitate the life of Jesus at all times. Jesus is described as the "Man for others." His love for His Father and His obedience to His Father's will were expressed in His giving of Himself for others. Read his famous teachings, the Beatitudes. Each of The Beatitudes calls us to "be for others."

So, knowing that, this is how the church and other people fit in to the whole picture of faith. God saves individuals to be in community with Him and the other people He's saved. I've often found that people who avoid church because they're "not holy enough" are judging other people in the church. How? By the simple fact they're thinking that the standard of entry into the church is holiness. If that were the case, we'd all be in trouble.

When you go to church, you're sitting with liars, adulterers, thieves, religious (in a bad way) and other sin addicts. Not one of us "belongs" there, but we're all there by the mercy of God. That is not only a direct challenge to our pride but also how we think about others. The very thought that we don't belong there should help us be merciful to those who feel they don't belong there either. I certainly don't "belong" being a priest. I'm here because God wants me here.

The parable that always drives this home for me comes from Jesus' parable in Matthew 18:21-35. If you're not familiar with the story, allow me to give you a rundown. A servant owes his master a crazy amount of money. Think millions of dollars with no way to pay it back. The servant begs his master for forgiveness and he forgives the debt.

So, what do you think the servant does? He goes out to find a fellow servant who owes him a very small amount of money. Do you think the guy forgives his fellow servant? Nope. He calls the authorities and has the fellow servant thrown in jail.

The master finds out what happened and calls the servant to task. He has the ungrateful servant thrown into the deepest, darkest dungeon where there is "weeping and gnashing of teeth."

Scary, isn't it? Jesus lays it out right there; to those who show mercy, mercy will be shown. Those who don't will be thrown into suffering, or hell, if you will.

———

I'm always amazed at how our outrage can turn to bitterness and hate. Someone told me a story about Robert E. Lee when a Kentucky woman confronted him after the war.

She said, "Those Yankees fired a cannon and destroyed my tree. Isn't that terrible? Aren't they just awful people? I hate them so much. They destroyed my beautiful tree, and I hope they all rot."

She looked at the general, expecting him to share her hatred and bitterness toward "the Yankees."

The white-haired general bowed to her and said, "Madam, cut down the tree and move on."

I love this story because it illustrates the power of forgiveness and how sin can destroy our relationships with others.

Whom did Jesus eat with? Sinners! Whom did Jesus care for? Sinners! With whom did Jesus associate? Sinners! Our churches were not built only for the convenience of saints. Our churches, like hospitals, are built to house and care for the sick and the infirm. A church is a place that we enter in order to find spiritual healing and wholeness for our souls.

When we harbor anger and bitterness toward our fellow sinners, it's like the diabetic wanting to beat up on the cancer patient for being "sicker" than they are.

We attend church on the weekends (and, hopefully, daily) because we need healing and wholeness. We attend church because we are sinners who need God's help through Christ's tender, loving mercies. We come to church not because we are hypocrites but because we are being honest with ourselves and honest with God. You cannot be a hypocrite and, at the same time, face the truth about yourself. We need that community of fellow hypocrites and sinners to remind us of our own sin. In that reminder, we can find God's grace and mercy.

Remember John 8:1-10. The woman caught in adultery was dragged before Jesus in her nakedness and shame. The woman became a pawn in the Pharisees' game with Jesus. Their own hearts were full of "this sin" as Jesus calls it, but they wanted to condemn this woman. The teachers of the law thought Jesus would either condemn her to be stoned to death, or tell her that sin wasn't really that big a deal. Either way, the Pharisees thought, we have Jesus trapped.

Instead, Jesus said to the crowd, "Hey, if you're completely innocent of sin, start throwing."

Seems kind of strange doesn't it? But Jesus knew their hearts. He knew they all had either committed adultery in deed or in their hearts. The Bible tells us that everyone in the crowd dropped their stones and walked away.

What is the point?

Jesus is the only one who had the right to condemn this woman. He is the only true innocent. Instead, He wraps his cloak around her and says, "I don't condemn you. Now go, and sin no more."

The woman experienced the forgiveness of God. The One who would be forsaken by all, except that very small group who stood at the foot of the Cross, would not abandon this woman. That is why she could not abandon Him. She transformed from a sinner into a follower of Christ through His grace.

Of all the people the Lord had contact with, thousands and thousands, He picked a repentant criminal dying on the cross next to Him to be the first to join Him in heaven. And He picked this woman, Mary Magdalene, to be the first to experience His resurrection. He chose her not because she had been a sinner, but because she trusted in Him.

Jesus will not abandon us. He loves us too much to leave us to our own devices. He continually prods us with our conscience, with the grace of the church, the encouragement and needs of our families, and the moral demands of our society. Our compassionate, loving Lord is more concerned with each of us as individuals than with the results of our sins. We just have to recognize our sins and do our best to fight off sin in the future. That's all He wants for us: to be cleansed, to be absolved. Even more, we must forgive those who trespass against us.

There are tremendous reflections on everyday life contained in the Gospels. Jesus is the solution to the problem of life. He is the one who will never abandon us. His presence in our lives is infinitely more important than anything else we hold onto: stones of anger and hatred, stones that actually hold us back from the Lord of Life.

I am here to tell you not to allow any person — whether a priest, minister, family member, friend — or past sins, to keep you away from the presence of Jesus. You are responsible for your soul. Take that responsibility seriously, as God will take His accountability of you seriously. When you do, you can love other people and God's church. The reason? You'll be so concerned about loving Christ that you'll forgive the hurts that people have inflicted upon you. When you love Christ, you can truly love others as you've been loved.

Are You Jesus Enough?

A few years ago, I was heading to a National Clergy Conference in Chicago. I assured my secretary and staff that I would be home in plenty of time for Saturday morning's First Communion practice.

I arrived late to the airport, quickly got through security, and began a mad dash toward my gate. Not paying attention, I plowed into a woman, causing her to drop an armful of binders. Without so much as an "I'm sorry," I kept going and made my gate on time.

Right before I handed over my ticket, the Holy Spirit reminded me of a story I heard once of another man's mad dash through the airport.

During this man's rush, he knocked over an apple cart. Apples spilled everywhere. Not wanting to miss his flight, he hurried on to his gate. As he walked down the jet way, he felt the Holy Spirit tug at his heart. He thought about the apple cart owner and the spilled apples all over the floor. Conviction came and he turned around and went back to the gate agent.

"Can I help you, Sir?" she asked.

"Yeah, I can't make this flight because of an emergency. Could I get a later flight out of here?"

She gave him a concerned look and then said, "Sure, we can do that."

After she made the later flight possible, the man went back through the gate and saw the apples still littering the floor.

His heart went into his throat as he saw the owner of the cart: a blind girl groping around the floor for her apples. Business people, families, and tourists raced passed her without a second thought. They rushed to their gates, just as he did, and didn't stop to help her.

The man prayed, "God, please forgive me."

He started picking up the apples and placed them on her table, organizing her display. He picked out the bruised apples and set them in another basket. He then pulled out two, twenty dollar bills.

The man said to the young lady, "Here, please take these forty dollars for the damage I did. Are you okay?"

She nodded through her tears.

"I hope that I didn't spoil your day too badly. It wasn't my intent! I was in a rush and focused on trying to catch my flight. It's been a long day," he babbled, feeling completely terrible.

As he said goodbye to her and began to walk away, the girl called out, "Mister?"

He turned and walked back toward her.

"Can I help you, dear?"

She paused for a moment and then said, "Mister — are you Jesus?"

"Jesus?" the man responded with a chuckle. "No, I am nothing like Jesus, to be honest. Jesus is good, kind, caring, and loving, and would have never have bumped into your display in the first place."

The girl continued, "I only ask because I prayed for Jesus to help me gather the apples. I was afraid and lost, and knew that with my disability I could never find them. Jesus sent you to help me, so you are like Him."

He stood there, stunned, his moment of selfishness transformed by God's grace.

As I remembered that story, I took a deep breath and said, "All right, Lord, I get it."

I turned around, went back to the woman and said, "Ma'am, please forgive me. Let me help you pick up the binders."

I did, and guess what?

I missed my flight.

As I boarded the flight later that evening, thoughts raced through my brain.

Am I Jesus enough?

I knew the honest answer to be no, but that didn't change the lesson God taught me.

I often wonder if people mistake you for Jesus. This is our destiny as Christians, as Catholics — is it not? To be so much like Jesus that people cannot tell the difference, as we live and interact with a world that is often so blatantly blind to His love, life, and grace.

Each weekend, as Catholics, we profess our faith at Mass. We enter our sacred space, marking ourselves with the Sign of the Cross. As Christians, we often quote Scripture, carry our Bibles, or wear a cross around our neck. If we claim to know Jesus, we should live, walk, and act as Jesus would. For, you see, knowing Jesus is more than simply quoting Scripture and going to the church of your choice. It's actually incorporating and living the Word of God as life unfolds day to day — the good, the bad, and the indifferent.

When we feel forgotten, we need to remember Christ's Words — His gift of peace. As an Advocate, He will look for us when we are lost, console us when we are down, and will be there when we feel alone.

Each of us are the apple of God's eye, and there is no one among us who has not been bruised by a fall, a failed relationship, an addiction, an abuse, financial trouble, children who have fallen away from the faith — the list goes on. But we must remember that Christ stopped what He was doing and picked us up on a hill called Calvary and paid in full for our damaged fruit.

Emmanuel: God is with us.

Look At My Hands

You wonder if I love you,
and you wonder if I care for you.
How many nights have you wondered if
I think of you?

Well, look at my hands.
Look at my feet. Look at my side.
When you do, you'll see my heart.
I died for you — I died for you.
And I'd die again, because I love you!

You wonder if there's hope for you,
and you wonder if there's life for you.
You search everywhere for meaning.

Well, look at my hands.
Look at my feet. Look at my side.
When you do, you'll see my heart. I died
for you. I died for you. And I'd die again,
because I love you!

And you shall rise like Me and
live with Me forever. Yes, you shall
rise like Me and live with Me forever,
because I love you!

———

This was written by a young man who is currently on death row and is scheduled to be executed for the crimes that he committed. Talk about reconciliation! Talk about conversion! God is always at work in our lives. Never give up. Never retreat. Open your heart and recognize: He has already fought the fight, He has won the race, and He is here for us!

Cutting the Grass

My father loved cutting the grass, but I hated every minute of it. On one early Saturday morning during my senior year in high school, I woke up and decided to do a random act of kindness for my Dad. I would grit my teeth and cut the grass.

Full of myself and the good I would be doing, I ran outside and got out the lawnmower. I couldn't figure out how to turn the thing on, so I asked a neighbor to help me. We gave the engine a few quick pulls, and I began to cut.

Ten seconds later, my father ran outside in his boxers. He put his hands on his hips and screamed, "What the [content edited for the Christian nature of this book] are you doing?"

I cut off the engine and said, "Dad, I love you and wanted to cut the grass for you."

He shook his head. "No, I can't let you do that."

"But, Dad! I wanted to do something for you, so I thought I'd do what I hate the most. Cut the grass!"

He sighed. "Fine, you can cut the back, but not the front."

My face fell, and I lowered my eyes.

Dad touched my shoulders, and I looked up at him. "Jimmy, people can see the front grass, no one can see the back."

I nodded, still not getting it. My father could read me like a book, so he said, "Look at me Jimmy."

I did, and he said, "Jimmy, you love me, but you don't love cutting grass. And it shows."

Husbands and wives: If you don't love one another, it shows! Regardless of how you try to hide it or fake it — it shows!

Children and parents: if you don't love one another, it shows!

Priests of God and parishioners: if you don't love one another, it shows!

God showed each of us how much He loves us, by giving us His only Son. By sacrificing His only Son, Jesus.

How do we show our love back to Him? Do we live what we profess? Do we practice what we believe? Do we strive to be better, each and every day?

Be honest.

What do you love? Does it show in everything you do? Do you do things because you love doing them or because you have to do them? My father's words gave me a great attitude check and instruction for later in life. Learn to love what you're doing. People will notice, catch the passion and learn to seek what they'll love to do, too.

The Highway

A prayer before your prayer —

God, grant me the grace to sit still. That I may hear the spirit's silent song, ever flowing like a river deep within, singing my love for you.

In any program of self-recovery – whether it be AA, Weight Watchers, Al-Anon, or private therapy – "Naming, Claiming, Taming" are the steps people practice for their recovery. Any recovering addict will tell you it's a day-to-day practice, even at times a minute-by-minute practice.

This is a great way to view our recovery from sin and its destructive effects on our lives. We're all sin addicts, and recovering in Christ comes in day-to-day steps.

I've tried to apply these principles to my own life, especially toward my, er, speeding problem. On a daily basis I need to remind myself not to break the law and put other people's lives in danger.

One morning, I went to Louisville for a meeting. This seemed like a great time to practice my newfound commitment not to speed. I slowed down to seventy, the posted speed limit, and got in the right lane.

I tried to pray during this time, a way to moderate my need for speed. The problem came when car after car started to pass me in the left lane. First a red Porsche, then a blue Honda, and finally a pickup truck. They all flew by me at the speed of light, and I gripped the steering wheel.

Two more cars sped past me.

"This is nuts, I don't know if I can do this, Lord."

Three more cars.

Finally, moderation went out the window. I decided to go into deep prayer with the Lord and said, "Dear Lord, as I have struggled with my speeding, I have watched cars zoom by me. I pray that, if you wish for me to arrive at my destination quicker, that you send a car zooming past me at this very moment. Through Christ Our Lord, Amen." (Sign of the Cross)

As soon as I said "Amen," a car zoomed by me, and I replied, "Thank you, Lord!" I switched lanes and sped up to follow them. An unspoken bond formed between me and this speeding stranger on the highway. They put on their blinker, and I put on mine. They switched lanes and I switched lanes. I honked my horn and waved at them.

I didn't even bother to check our speed. All I knew was, as the mileage markers slipped by, that we made excellent time. The car went around a semi-truck and I followed.

Wheee! We're in this together, I thought.

The car pulled over into the median. I held up my hand in blessing and sped around them. I noticed the car speed up and pull up right behind me. A man pulled out a blue light and put it on top of the car.

"You've got to be kidding me," I said as I pulled over to the side of the road.

Two of the largest Kentucky State Troopers I'd ever seen got out of the car. These men looked like body builders, and they didn't look happy. In fact, I half expected them to pull out their guns.

They knocked on my window and I swallowed hard. I tried to put a smile on my face as I rolled down the window.

"Um, Father, do you mind telling us what the heck you think you were doing?"

"I, uh, I, well, I was following you to, um, make better time."

The Trooper frowned. "No, Father, you were chasing me while I was chasing a suspect."

I laughed. "Well, it looks like you got the wrong person."

Not very entertained by my joke, he pulled out his ticket book.

We chase the wrong things all the time, do we not?

Seriously, though, what is it in your life that you are following? What is it that you are chasing? And are some of the things you are following things that you ultimately should be chasing after?

We are called to be people of faith, trusting and believing in the Word of God. We are called to learn from our mistakes. We must take into account our weaknesses and use these as opportunities for growth, accountability, and, ultimately, evangelization.

We follow so many things. We follow sports figures. We follow politicians. We follow the priest or preacher who gives a fantastic sermon or serves the congregation well. All those things are good in and of themselves. Indeed, we should follow people when they personify Christ. But, all those people are human beings. This means a guarantee that they'll let us down in some form or fashion. The idea is to stop lifting up idols in the place of Christ and following those idols to destruction. Instead, we should follow the One who gave up His life for us and keep striving to demonstrate Him.

Again, we should look for godly role models. That's not the problem. It's okay to have a hero, as long as that hero does as Christ would do.

So, each weekend, as you enter your place of worship, you should be a different person — not the same person you were a week prior. A little bit changed for the better — challenged and moving forward on this journey called Life, being led by the Great Shepherd.

Dry Leaf and Mud Pie

There's an ancient Hindu parable about two characters: Dry Leaf and Mud Pie. They were very good friends. As they approached old age together, they decided to make a religious pilgrimage to Banaras, the Hindu holy city on the banks of the Ganges River.

They believed that if they washed in that sacred river, all the sins of their lifetime would be erased. They understood the distance and the dangers of such a trip. They knew that heavy rains and strong winds were the two greatest hazards they would face. So, they decided on a clever strategy. When the rains poured down, Dry Leaf would shield Mud Pie until the storm passed. When the heavy winds blew, Mud Pie would sit on Dry Leaf until the sandstorm was over.

One bright, sunny morning, Dry Leaf and Mud Pie set out on the long, difficult pilgrimage to the holy city of Banaras.

They traveled just a short distance when the sky grew dark and rain began to fall. Dry Leaf shielded Mud Pie until the rain stopped. Their strategy worked, and they laughed as they continued on their way.

As they got further down the road, the sky clouded again, but this time, the wind blew in with a terrible force. Mud Pie sat on Dry Leaf until the wind died down. Their strategy still worked, and as they traveled on, they started to sing.

They had gotten almost to the holy city before the sky clouded over again. Then something terrible happened. The rain poured down, and the wind blew — at the same time.   Although the two friends tried their best to help each other, it was of no use. Dry Leaf blew away and was never seen again. And Mud Pie was washed away.

I like this parable because it illustrates a very important point. There comes a time in life when no matter how much we are loved and helped by another, it's not enough. Even the love and support of our best friends can't help us. There'll come a time in your life, maybe more than once, when God's help will be your only refuge.

You see, many of the insights of the saints of our church stem from his or her experience as one who has fallen, one who has sinned, one who is able to recognize that he or she is a sinner.

Our Holy Father, Pope Francis, takes his name from St. Francis of Assisi. Everyone knows this saint as a humble man who followed Christ all of his life by helping the poor, caring for animals, and challenging the powerful. What many people don't know is that he was the son of a rich merchant who lived the wild life of a medieval party animal.

One day, he came face to face with the grinding poverty of the people around him. As he listened to their everyday faith in God, he realized his own spiritual poverty. Francis gave up his birthright and became a holy beggar.

There comes a time in life when God, and only God, can provide us with the kind of help that we need. We must always remember, "A saint is never consciously a saint; a saint is consciously dependent upon God."

This brings us to the Beatitudes we often hear proclaimed at weddings, funerals, and special liturgical celebrations. "Blessed are the poor in spirit, for theirs is the Kingdom of Heaven!"

To be "poor in spirit" means to realize the point shared in the Hindu parable: we must realize that without God in our lives, we are nothing. In other words, to be "poor in spirit" means to understand in a deeply personal way these memorable words from Scripture: "I am the vine, you are the branches; without me you can do nothing. Anyone who does not remain in me will be thrown out like a branch and wither" (John 15:5-6).

The literal translation of being poor in spirit means "spirit beggars." To be a beggar in Jesus' time carried the same social taboo as it does now. Every saint in the history of the church came to this point in their lives, realizing the great truth all followers of Christ comes to know. It is this great truth that was the secret of their happiness. They knew that without Jesus, they were spiritually poor. They filed their spiritual bankruptcy with God's bank.

And so these early Christians made it the number-one priority in their lives to stay united with Jesus. God calls us to do the same. Let us make sure we realize that this instruction does not mean that we are called to go forth and do big, heroic things, but to live our lives in what we profess in the faith we confess.

When Mother Teresa still lived with us on this earth, I got to meet her and her sisters. The first time, I met them in New York City and the second time in Rome. Each time, I felt so inspired by their example I said to them, "Mother and Sisters, I think God might be calling me to join you in your work."

Mother took my hand and stared me in the eyes. "No, Father, it's an illusion. Go back to Kentucky, go back home and serve the poor in your own diocese."

I'd gotten so caught up in seeing the work in other lands, that I didn't see the opportunities right in front of me. Mother Teresa taught me a huge lesson and wiped the stars from my eyes.

And that is the message I believe, for all of us. Regardless of where we are in our lives, regardless of how faithful we may be, we are called to bloom where we are planted. We are called to cultivate the soil through the Sacrament of Reconciliation and grace, and live honestly our own Baptismal call.

As a priest, my call is to serve God through the church. Very few people should take up this call unless they've prayed, discerned and joined in consultation with their own parish priest and their bishop. Does this mean my call is greater than anyone else's? Not at all.

God may call you to be a teacher, a construction worker, a doctor, a grocery store manager or a yogurt stand worker. All of these calls are equal in His Eyes and they've got a grand purpose in His design. There is no such thing as a "lesser call." God puts us in the places He wishes for a reason.

What is our job? We're supposed to cultivate, educate and develop the talents He gives us. He wants us to see where we can serve Him in the here and now. We, His saints, are made to be servants in everything we do.

So, ask yourself, "What has God given me to do? Where can I serve Him where I am? How can I serve Him in my life?"

Lead Like a Shepherd

J esus calls himself The Good Shepherd. We might even say He is The Shepherd; the One who defines what every person who leads others should seek to imitate. In our time, we call this a "leader," and many of us are called to leadership in different areas of our lives.

My bishop, Ronald Gainer, taught me six principles of leadership that I talk about in all my travels. I think they apply to any area where you might lead; whether it's your family, your work, your town or in your faith.

These six points of leadership have been discovered and paired with Jesus' life throughout Scripture.

Anchoring

A leader and a shepherd possess an internal anchor. No matter what happens, they are rooted, and nothing will shake them. Yes, a natural "swaying" happens from time to time. But they remain rooted. We see that in Jesus Christ.

Jesus' internal anchor arose from the work He came to do in obedience to His Father. We read in the Gospels about the constant dialogue between Jesus and the Father. When Jesus got tired, stressed and overwhelmed (the Gospels tell us that happened a lot), He went into the mountains to be with His Father.

In the Garden, Jesus sweated blood as he faced the unimaginable suffering of the next day. He said, "Father, if it's possible, take this cup from me; yet not my will, but Yours be done."

The conviction of these words sustained Christ as he went through the pain of the cross and separation from His father at the moment of His death.

When He rose from the dead, Jesus became our internal anchor. He roots us in the love and will of the Father. When we face storms, trials, sufferings, or anything that might cause us to sway from the path of God, Jesus remains like a rock during the storm.

Christian leaders must find their anchoring in Christ. Why? Without Him, our leadership will come apart in the storm and crash against the rocks. Not only will we take ourselves down, but we'll take others down with us.

Attitude of Gratitude

Every time Jesus prepared himself to heal, eat, or go about His Father's business, Jesus gave thanks. And so should a good leader. You should give thanks. Husbands, you should thank your wives. Wives, you should thank your husbands. Children, you should thank your parents and your teachers. Employees, you should thank your bosses and those you are called to serve.

Have a simple attitude of gratitude; far too often we deflect that thanks. Sometimes after Mass, a parishioner will say, "Oh, Father, the homily was great." And, because I'm too self-conscious, I will deflect that compliment by saying something like, "Well, I thought it went too long, didn't you?"

Just say, "Thank you!"

"Gosh, Father, have you lost weight? You look great!" And I'll say, "No, actually, I've gained twenty pounds. I'm just wearing larger clothes."

Just say, "Thank you!"

"I love your haircut!" And I'll say, "She cut it too short, don't you think?"

Just say, "Thank you!"

Receive it! Have an openness of heart!

I've often found that the above comments might seem like humility. They aren't. All those comments do is draw more attention to us and not to Christ. When we just accept compliments in humility, then Christ is glorified in our work.

When I was seventeen, my mother's doctor discovered a brain tumor in the lower part of her head. Back then, they shaved the entire head before surgery. When she got home, we purchased a beautiful wig for her. She hated the thing and thought it made her look ugly.

One day, we took her shopping at the local grocery store. Some friends saw her and came up to us.

"Marie, you look amazing. We're so glad the surgery went well, you don't even look sick. Thank God. We really love what you've done with your hair."

My mother grabbed her hair and pulled off the wig as she said, "It's a wig, see?"

I whispered out of the corner of my mouth, "Just say 'thank you,' Mom."

Leaders lead in gratitude, saying thanks without making a huge deal out of things. In this, you'll show grace not only under fire, but under praise. Believe it or not, that's probably the harder of the two.

Have the humility to know when people thank you for something; they are really thanking your anchor, Christ. Accept it and move on.

Keeper of the Vision

A good leader, a good shepherd, is a keeper of the vision. As a pastor, I am called to keep those who follow the faith on track within the Catholic faith.

Sometimes, my parishioners may say to me, "Father, let's have a social here in the sacred space of the church and have coffee and donuts before Mass." And, as keeper of the vision, I say, "No, no, we can't do that, because this is a sacred space."

The Evil One invited Jesus to lose the vision after His fast in the desert. He said, "Turn these stones to bread. Throw yourself off this temple. Deviate from the Father's plan."

Each time, Jesus answered with the words of His Father from Scripture. He defeated the enemy by keeping the vision of the Father.

A good leader not only keeps the vision but also communicates the vision. Jesus communicated the vision by telling stories, by giving parables, by challenging people. We are all called to communicate the vision, the Gospel, the faith of Jesus Christ, and the Roman Catholic Church. We don't always have to communicate it by word of mouth. We can communicate it with actions. For example, by giving thanks. When eating with family, whether it is at a restaurant or at home, we mark ourselves with the Sign of the Cross, and we give the blessing.

We can communicate the vision in our response to receiving an inappropriate email at work. We can avoid gossip about the new woman or man in the office. We can close our ears to unfounded complaints or attempts to tear down other people's character.

You might say, Father, this isn't easy. People don't like it when you act weird like that. They just want you to be normal. You know, you're right, they do. People don't like the truth. You don't like the truth. Yet, the truth is real and guides our lives in Christ.

Here's the thing. Jesus spoke the truth, and most people hate it. Should we expect anything different?

Willing to Do Difficult Things

Jesus loved to associate with the outcasts — the people shunned by society. Believe it or not, He even associated with religious hypocrites who pointed their fingers at others. He took twelve malcontents (we call them apostles now), screw-ups, and deniers of Him, to make them leaders of his new Kingdom. Finally, He took up His cross, bore our sins, and died a terrible death.

And so too, parents, as leaders of your family, you're called to be parents first. That means that your child may not always like you — but you're not called to be their friends, you're called to be their parents. You're going to be called to do difficult things. Your child may not always want to go to church, but do you know what you do? You pick your child up and you drag him to church. Your child may not want to look both ways before crossing the street either, but you make her.

This isn't a popular idea, but it must be done. Sometimes, making people do something is the only way to get them to see.

You teach them. You be a parent.

Look for the "Smalls"

Being a leader means that small things matter — like simply encouraging someone, sending a note, saying "thank you," and being kind.

Many of you may not know this, but those who follow me on Facebook or Twitter might. Recently, I hired a personal trainer, who, for three days a week causes me undue pain in my life.

I've honestly considered going to therapy to help me understand why I would put myself through such pain. Even more, why would anyone pay for someone else to inflict pain on them?

The only reason I do this, to be honest with you, is so that I can lift the heavy gospel books we use in Mass.

One day, we worked out, and then my trainer handed me a sixty-pound weight. He tells me to pick it up and put it down, pick it up and put it down. So, up and down I go with this weight, while he reminds me: "Keep your back straight! Be mindful of your posture!"

Finally, I say, "I can't do this."

He says, "Yes you can!"

I say, "No, I can't!"

He says, "Yes, you can! And you will! Now give me twenty-five!"

So I keep going, up and down, up and down, and then I dropped the weight on his foot!

He howled in pain and fell to the ground. I picked him up, threw his arm around my shoulder and took him to the car.

As I drove him to the hospital, I fought the urge to say, "Remember, like you tell me, keep focused. You can get through it. Now, practice your breathing. Deep breaths. Come on. You can do it."

While the nurse carted him off to the X-ray room, I went to Baskin Robbins. I got us both mint chocolate chip ice cream, and we ate while they put on his cast.

I'm always amazed how small things like that transform people. A few lines of a note to thank someone for bringing me bread. I give a word from the pulpit to thank the ladies who wash the sacramental linens every week. It doesn't take much for people to feel appreciated, loved and valued.

I learned this from Jesus.

Our Lord traveled far on His journey with many places yet to go and many people still to see. During these times, He always noticed the small things and small people.

In a well-known story from the Gospels, masses of people gathered around Jesus. Instead of noticing the many, He noticed someone else.

He saw Zacchaeus, the tax collector, hanging from the tree. Why was Zacchaeus up there? Zacchaeus couldn't push his way through the crowd to see Jesus. So, he did the natural thing and looked for the highest place possible.

And what did Jesus do? Jesus stopped, and He looked up and invited Zacchaeus to come down with Him. Jesus didn't have to do that, but He did because He realized that small things matter. He went to have dinner with Zacchaeus and transformed him all because Jesus simply noticed.

In another instance, amidst a crowd of thousands upon thousands of followers who pressed in around Jesus, a woman reached out and touched the hem of Jesus' garment. Jesus knew who touched him. He knew His power healed the woman in an instant. Yet, He didn't want to call her out in front of the crowd. Instead, He said, "Who touched me?" And He didn't do this to embarrass the woman. He did this to give that woman dignity. He did this to give that woman a sense of happiness and fulfillment.

When you're a leader, your job is to give people worth and recognition. Find ways to give it them, lift them up, and never degrade them to make yourself look better. Anyone who does that is not a leader, and certainly is not a follower of Christ. Don't be that guy or girl, as the kids say.

A Leader Doesn't Depend Upon the Approval of Others

All leaders attract followers, but they don't depend on them. Could you imagine if Jesus placed the whole dependence of His call on His twelve disciples? Could you imagine that?

Judas?

Thomas?

Even Peter?

What about James and John squabbling over wanting to be his "right hand" guy?

And neither should we! If my priesthood depended upon whether my home parish liked me or not, I would have been gone within my first three weeks — probably within two!

The disciples learned this from Jesus and, with the power of the Spirit, helped spread the Gospel into the world — because they didn't rely on the approval of the Roman Empire.

Ask yourself: Are you a leader of Jesus? Are you a leader of the faith? Are you a leader of your baptismal call? Or, are you just a follower? Are you just doing the routine — because the routine is what you have always done?

There is a difference between those who lead and those who follow. We have seen them. We know them. And I challenge them — and I challenge you —to step up to the plate.

For those called to lead, keep in mind: A leader...

1. Has an internal anchor
2. Shows gratitude
3. Is a keeper of the vision and communicates the vision
4. Is willing to do difficult things
5. Knows that small things matter
6. Will attract followers but does not rely on those followers

Intentions

I'd like to share a story of a priest friend of mine. He struggled with his parish and they struggled with him. They couldn't seem to get it together.

One woman in particular in the parish, who attended daily Mass, decided to shout out her daily intention when my friend would open up the Mass for whispered prayer. Every day she would yell, "For a special intention, we pray to the Lord!"

After many weeks of repeating this routine, this woman took ill. As she lay on her deathbed, my friend and I went to see her. After we prayed for her, my friend decided he couldn't resist.

"I've got to ask, what was your special intention, so I can pray for it when you go to be with the Lord?"

The woman stared him square in the face and said, "My special intention was that you would be transferred."

Ask and you shall receive, seek and you shall find, knock and the door will be opened.

However, one of the things that we fail to notice in this popularly quoted Scripture verse is that the Lord never tells us what we will receive. He never shares which door we knock on will be opened, or that we will find exactly what we seek. The Lord does share that in our asking, seeking, and finding, He will be present to respond and answer. Even more interesting, He promises to be with us as we seek. If you think about it, that is the more comforting promise, because most of our lives are spent seeking answers.

It's not about us. It's about Him. Everything about us, all our stories, beliefs, movements, and actions should always lead to Jesus.

———

My office sits facing toward the busy intersection of Main Street located in the heart of our city. I looked out my window one day and saw a man being tailgated by a woman. It reminded me of a story I'd heard about something similar.

There was a man being tailgated by a stressed-out woman. Suddenly, the light turned yellow just in front of him. He did the right thing and stopped at the crosswalk, even though he could have beaten the red light by accelerating through the intersection. The tailgating woman was furious. Dropping her cell phone and makeup, she honked her horn, screaming in frustration as she missed her chance to get through the intersection. She was still mid-rant when she heard a tap on her window, and a very serious police officer (who happened to be a parishioner of mine) ordered her to exit her car. He took her to the police station where she was searched, fingerprinted, photographed, and placed in the Detention Center.

After a couple of hours, a policeman approached the cell and opened the door. She was escorted back to the booking desk where the arresting officer was waiting with her personal effects.

He said to her, "I'm very sorry for this mistake. You see, I pulled up behind your car while you were blowing your horn, flipping off the guy in front of you, and cussing a blue streak. I noticed the bumper stickers that said What Would Jesus Do? and Follow Me to St. Mark School, the Choose Life license plate holder, and the chrome-plated

Christian fish emblem on the trunk, so I assumed you stole the car."

I have no idea if this story is true, but it reminded me that people are always watching those of us who confess faith in Christ. Always.

West Nile Virus

Years ago, my mother contracted West Nile virus and became very sick. In fact, I can't remember ever seeing my mom that bad until her near-death experience. While she lay in bed, I did my best to see her every week.

I would say my weekend Masses in Kentucky, and then on Sunday nights I would fly to Houston to be with my mother until Saturday morning. Then I would fly from Houston back to Kentucky. I did this through July, August, September, and October. On my last day, after my mother got well enough to be on her own, I made the last trip from Houston to Kentucky.

Of course, it was a 5:45 a.m. flight, US Airways out of Intercontinental Airport, going from Houston to Pittsburgh, Pittsburgh to Lexington. I got on the flight, sat in my same seat as I always do, you know — 12A emergency exit window. Being that early, I didn't feel like one of Jesus' sunbeams. I didn't even put on my clericals that morning.

As I watched the people board the plane, I noticed a young

man about 22-years-old, wearing all-camouflage, with braided hair that flowed everywhere, the biggest grin on his face, and a rainbow-colored knit hat.

And I said to myself, Don't You dare do it! Don't You do it, Lord— not today!

And this man was just hoping — he looked around and said, "Emergency exit 12B! That's me!"

He sat down, and I whispered, "Thank you for listening..."

The man looked at me and said, "Dude . . . dude . . . dude."

And when I finally turned to look at him, he said, "Morning!"

I just kind of looked at him and nodded a silent hello.

The man kept going. "Hey! Morning!"

I mustered a small voice in return, hoping not to encourage him and said, "Hello."

He said, "Well, you're sure not the talkative one!"

I told the man, "No, I just want to relax and be by myself, okay?"

"Dude . . . dude . . . do you want to share, man? Open your heart, man! Come on — share!"

I looked at him and said, "You don't want to know what I want to share right now..."

He turned to me and said, "Oh! Turn that frown upside down! Come on, man!"

I used one of my escape methods. I said, "Well, I think I'm going to take a little nap." Then, I just kind of leaned my head on the window and pretended to fall asleep. I almost made a snoring noise but decided that would've been a bit much.

As our flight took off, he hit me, saying, "Dude . . . dude . . . look at this, man! We're like a bird up in the sky! We are flying high! Woohoo! What do you think about that!?"

I said to him, "I don't think this plane is the only thing flying high right now."

He said, "Dude, chill. Take a chill pill, and be still. Relax."

The man continued to persist with, "Dude . . . dude."

So I did the second thing I usually do to deter unwanted talkers on a plane. I put on my earphones! (It is important to note that I don't bring a music player when I travel.)

So, when he continued to talk, I pointed to my earphones and shrugged, signifying that I couldn't hear what he said over the music.

The man tapped me on the shoulder, "Dude . . . dude." He picked up the cord from my headphones and said, "You're not connected to anything! Man, what are you listening to?! There's nothing connected! Dude! Man, I'd like to hear that music!"

Then he hit me and said, "Dude, they're coming down with the grub cart! You want some?"

I finally reached my limit. I said, "You know what I want? I want you to move! This is US Airways! They're going bankrupt! There is no one on this flight! But you are sitting right next to me! Could you just move to give me some space!?"

He seemed taken aback and said, "Hmm, you are an angry fellow, aren't you?"

The plane landed in Pittsburgh. I pushed the man out of my way and ran through the airport! I ran to the gate so I could catch my next flight.

I looked at the "Arrivals/Departures" monitor, and it said, Lexington, KY— Delayed.

I talked to the woman at the counter, and I said, "Excuse me, but my name is Father Jim Sichko. I know I don't look like a priest today, but I am a priest. I'd like to know why the flight is delayed."

She said to me, "Father, the reason the flight is delayed is because we are overbooked by one passenger."

I forced a smile and said, "Ma'am, let me tell you something. I have to get back to Lexington, because I am scheduled to say Mass this evening at Mary Queen of the Holy Rosary. God just told me that I need to be on this flight." (I joked with her to put some fun into it.) "And if someone doesn't put me on that flight, then someone is going..." I pointed down to where there is a much warmer climate.

This woman's eyes widened. She looked at me as if I gave her a death sentence. Just as she opened her mouth, I got a tap on my shoulder from none other than...

"Dude . . . dude . . . dude."

My own eyes got enormous!

I turned around, and, lo and behold, there stood the man in camouflage who had driven me insane during the last flight!

What do you think he said to me?

He said, "Dude . . . dude, clarify something for me. Did I just hear you say you're a Catholic priest?"

Upon hearing this, I went from my six-foot-two-inch height down to two-inches tall.

I nodded, "Yes, you heard correct — I am a Catholic priest."

The guy said, "Dude — did I hear correct that you have to get to Lexington to say Mass?"

I told the man, "Yes, you heard correct."

The man turned to the woman behind the counter and said, "Ma'am, give him my seat. I can wait."

The face of Jesus became so real to me in the face of this stranger. I began to cry, and I took my next step to admit my surly attitude.

I went up to that man and said, "Sir, I'm sorry. I'm sorry, because the way I treated you is not only not the way a priest should treat someone, but not even the way a human being should treat someone. I'm sorry."

He looked at me and said, "Dude . . . relax! Do you have family in Houston?"

I said, "Yes I do."

He smiled. "It's okay, then. We'll fly again sometime!"

No, we won't! No, thank you!

I nodded. "Well, I just wanted you to know that I'm sorry."

It's all about recognizing Christ! It's all about recognizing that we aren't in control! We must realize that every one of us is going to make a mistake. Every one of us is going to have difficulties. It's about recognizing that, even in our weaknesses, Christ is there. It's about understanding, even as we struggle with new job opportunities, or struggle within our church parish, God is still there.

Let me share something with you. God is a big God. Stop doing all the worrying for Him! He's going to take care of it! He's going to take care of us! There is no need for us to start criticizing one another and pointing fingers. Realize and recognize that God is always with us!

The L Words

1. Lord
2. Live
3. Love
4. Listen
5. Learn
6. Laugh
7. Labor
8. Lead
9. Leisure
10. Legacy

Take a look at these ten L's and see where you resonate. Regardless of your occupation in life, you go for success. Mediocrity is the Devil's playground.

Second Time's
a Conversion

I love driving, and even though I may not be good at it, I enjoy a
long trip in the car. Recently, as I traveled on Interstate 55 through
Mississippi on my way to Texas (you guessed it), I got pulled over
for speeding by a Mississippi State Trooper. The trooper issued me a
"warning," and I went on my way.

After spending a week with my mother, it was time to head back
up to Kentucky, so naturally, I took the same route to return home.

And I got pulled over again!

I looked up at the trooper, who stood with a menacing look near
my window, and he asked that I exit the vehicle. I proceeded to the
rear of the vehicle, and the trooper looked at me with a perplexed look.

He said, "Don't I know you? You look familiar!"

I gave him a slightly peevish grin and said, "Well, helloooo! You
should know me — you pulled me over last week as I was going in the

116

opposite direction!"

"What type of work do you do?"

I replied, "You'll never believe it. I'm a priest — a Catholic priest!"

His eyes opened wide, and he smiled. "Wow, I have seriously been trying to figure out if I am being called to the Catholic faith. I've even gone so far as visiting with my parish priest. Could I ask you a question? Would you have a few moments to visit if your schedule permits it? There is a coffee shop up at the next exit!"

I pondered a moment and then replied, "It all depends."

Here, once again, an amazing opportunity that God seemed to work, even in the midst of something not so comical or pleasing.

We became friends. Two years later I joined the trooper and his family on Holy Saturday night in a church right outside of Jackson, Mississippi. They were all baptized and confirmed, and he received his First Holy Communion — all Sacraments of Initiation into the Roman Catholic faith.

We are taught that every moment is a teachable moment. The fact is God wants to be found in each of our experiences of daily living. He provides us so many opportunities — even at the most unexpected times. When we travel through even the darkest tunnels of our lives, we may come out the other side. We might find a transforming experience, and encounter the holy.

It might be on a mountain. On the highway. At the spa. Or it might be in the next cubicle at work. It might be watching a toddler learning to walk or hearing a kind word from a stranger or friend who happens to be in your presence.

God is present. If we only look, we will find Him.

This Mississippi State Trooper reminded me of the limitless possibilities of God — One God, who cannot ever be contained or placed "in a box." God is ready to help us, because He is a God who wants to be found in the everyday experiences of our lives.

Besides not being a morning person and working on my speedometer, I am also one who is not so good with names. Recently, while I was at Central Baptist Hospital to anoint an elderly parishioner, I was waiting on an elevator when around the corner came a young man in his late twenties.

He immediately screamed out: "Father Jim, I can't believe you're here!"

I thought to myself, Who is this man?

He then exclaimed, "My wife, not fifteen minutes ago, gave birth to our second child! You must come up right now and bless our new baby!"

As I was trying to figure out who this man was, and let him know I was heading to ICU to anoint a parishioner, the elevator doors opened. He shoved me inside and pressed the second floor button.

"My wife will never believe that you are here, she is going to be floored!"

I exclaimed to myself, Who is this man that just kidnapped a priest at Central Baptist!

I followed him down the hall. He knocked on the door of a hospital room, and immediately as I walked in, this little second-grader came running from behind the door.

This little boy screamed out, "Wow, Father Jim is here!" and he hugged me around my legs!

I screamed to myself, Who is this boy? Who are these people? Who is this family?

Out of the corner of my eye, I saw this fifteen-minute-old child in the arms of his mother. I hadn't ever seen this before. As I walked closer to the bed, I immediately began to say aloud, "Jesus." And then I said it again, even louder, "Jesus," and again, "Jesus."

Immediately, while hitting my leg, the little second-grade boy screamed out, "That isn't Jesus! Jesus is a boy baby, that's a girl baby. This is Jesus' sister!"

Listen to the words of this little guy. He knew his baby sister belonged to Jesus in some way as a part of His family. What if we saw each other that way? What if we treated our neighbors with that sort of insight; that Jesus' brother or sister is standing in front of us? Would we be so quick to throw out the finger when someone cuts us off on the highway? Would we be so quick to spread that malicious gossip? My guess would be, no, we wouldn't.

Pope Francis, our new Holy Father, is challenging the whole church to reach out to people around them. He wants bishops, priests and lay people to get out into their communities. In other words, he wants us to see Jesus in all of our conversations, all of our friends, our family and, wait for it . . . our enemies. The Holy Father is telling the clergy to "smell like the sheep."

You may not be shepherds, but you can smell like the sheep in your own life.

Death

The word for "death" in German is Heimgen, which translates literally into "going home." In French, it is au ciel, which means, "until we meet in heaven." In English, goodbye is one of the saddest words in our native tongue.

We learn that "to die" means that we physically leave this life on earth, but we also "live" in the hearts of those we leave behind. You see, the French and the German languages have it right. Even though those who died are not physically with us, they are still with us. Spiritually, mentally, through our stories of them, through our experiences, through what we learned from them, through how they affected our lives, in our hearts, in the core of our very beings, they live on.

This past week, I got called out of town to honor the death of a neighbor who truly was the "life of the party!" This woman, though relatively young at the age of sixty-two, died unexpectedly in her sleep. She enjoyed life to the fullest. You could always find her in the summer months poolside at the local country club, with a Miller Lite in her hand. She knew everything going on and everyone who was passing by — that was Sandye.

Even though Sandye was Episcopalian (a.k.a. Catholic Lite!), her family asked me to preside over and preach at her memorial service. I shared with my mother about the family's request for me to preach, and my mother spoke the words that I thought in my head, What an honor!

As a priest, it's my "job." The ministry provides me an opportunity to baptize the infants, offer prayers of healing to the sick, witness the marriage of couples, and bury the dead. When Sandye's family asked me to preside at her funeral, I felt like they gave me a gift to honor someone who gave so much.

I use a lot of props when I preach. It's my style. Usually, I keep my "prop" hidden in my vestments. Let me tell you, I've taken hiding things to a whole new art form.

I began the funeral service by revealing a crucifix and speaking of the love of Christ in Sandye's life, and vice versa. Next, I pulled out a bottle of suntan lotion, followed by little bottles of water from the pool where Sandye would sit almost daily. Eyes grew in wonder and amazement as the ushers came forward, providing each guest with a sample of pool water with Sandye's name on it, as well as her date of birth and the date of her entrance into eternal life.

Some eyes opened even more widely, in shock, as I pulled out a bottle of Bud Lite. I knew it was not Sandye's favorite beer. I spoke of her passing on the previous day in Lexington, and a distributor, who did not even know Sandye, decided to make it a gift for me to use in this service.

Again the ushers came forward, this time with bottles of Bud Lite for everyone in attendance. I'm very sure Sandye watched every moment and laughed with Jesus about "crazy" Father Sichko. I hoped it would honor her memory.

After the service, I heard comments from individuals such as, "We entered mourning the loss of a friend but left celebrating and happy that we experienced her life!" and, "This is exactly what funerals should be: a celebration of the true person."

I noticed that the person last in line happened to be Sandye's parish priest. I shuddered, wondering what he thought during the entire service.

I didn't have to wait long to find out.

He approached me and asked to speak with me in private. As we talked, he led us into the sacristy, which is about the most private area of a church.

I knew some eyebrows rose during such an unusual and "in your face" eulogy honoring a woman who lived large.

The priest looked at me and said, "Do you mind if I ask you a question?"

Fearing that I faced an eventual fraternal correction, all I could say was, "Continue."

The priest asked, "Do you have an extra bottle of Bud Lite? And a bottle of pool water? I wanted to put them in remembrance of Sandye, here in the sacristy."

I knew it would be hard to pull off or accomplish such a eulogy before hundreds of people who know me as "Jimmy" instead of "Father." These people might easily perceive my tribute as irreverent.

Instead, everyone — including Sandye's Episcopalian priest — showed graciousness and openness. They received with open hearts, the many gifts that God provides us through Scripture and the Holy Spirit. They demonstrated the ability to trust, to risk, and to be persons of faith in the midst of hope.

We take so much for granted and rarely stop to be grateful for that which we have received.

Sandye's untimely death had shocked all of us into focusing on the here and now, realizing those powerful words of Scripture, which remind us, that tomorrow may never come, and that today is truly a gift that is given. Even in the prayer that we dare to recite and know all too well, the Our Father/Lord's Prayer, Jesus clearly says that Our Father will provide us our daily bread — not a month's supply or even a week's supply, but only enough to get through today.

Remember Matthew 6:25-34:

Therefore I tell you, do not be anxious about your life, what you will eat or what you will drink, nor about your body, what you will put on. Is not life more than food, and the body more than clothing? Look at the birds of the air: they neither sow nor reap nor gather into barns, and yet your heavenly Father feeds them. Are you not of more value than they? And which of you by being anxious can add a single hour to his span of life? And why are you anxious about clothing? Consider the lilies of the field, how they grow: they neither toil nor spin, yet I tell you, even Solomon, in all his glory was not arrayed like one of these.

Even though my schedule only permitted me to fly down and spend a few hours to preside over Sandye's memorial service, I knew I needed to make the time. Even if it meant canceling important meetings on the calendar for weeks, or a luncheon with a friend heading into town. It reminded me that being a true friend does not depend on my own needs, but truly on the needs of others.

Once we get so consumed with "I" or with "me," then we start to ignore one of the most challenging and difficult teachings of Jesus: "Whatever you do to the least of my brothers and sisters, you do to Me."

Today, I celebrate the Life of Sandye. Though she is no longer with us physically, she is definitely among us in spirit, memories, and laughter!

Cheers!

Weed Man

I like things neat, nice, and organized. One spring day, I walked out to the parish parking lot, and I saw weeds sprouting up in every crack! They were everywhere! Let me tell you, as my father could attest, God rest his soul, I know nothing about lawns and grass.

I called the number to a business that, believe it or not, is called "Weed Man." So, within a few days, the Weed Man came out to see me. They arrived in this big truck, and in bold lettering the truck read, "WEED MAN."

Needless to say, it caught the attention of a lot of college students in my parish. I'm sure they got a great chuckle out of it in private.

They couldn't help but smile as they asked, "Hey, Father — do you know the Weed Man?"

I said, "Yeah, he came to my house."

When the Weed Man did come, he wore a long face as if someone hit my dog. He said in a low, sorrowful voice, "Father, I'm sorry, but I'm not able to help you. Your weeds are weeds. Nothing that I do is going to help."

I stood there, hands at my side, and watched as this guy almost broke into tears.

"So what are you saying?"

He said, "I'm not going to be able to help you. You're going to just have to deal with those weeds being there."

Then he left.

I stood on my front porch, not sure what had just happened.

I thought, the Weed Man advertises that he can get rid of weeds, but he just told me he can't get rid of my weeds.

A neighbor lady approached me and said, "You have a weed problem?"

I responded, "Well, how do you know that?"

"The whole neighborhood knows. The Weed Man was just here."

I admitted to the woman, "Yes, I do have a weed problem."

The woman pointed down a hill in the near distance. "Did you notice that there are little bits of green grass down there?"

I said, "Yes, I've noticed that, but there are tons of weeds."

She looked at me and said, "Why don't you focus on the grass instead of focusing on the weeds? Why don't you give a little love and nurturing to the grass and ignore the weeds?"

The weeds disappeared and the grass returned.

You see, I hope this book will help with the weed problems in your life. Weeds grow up in all our lives. The weeds of sin, the weeds of loneliness, the weeds of self-loathing, because we think God or other people can never love us.

Why do we focus on the negative within ourselves? Why not focus on the positive and allow the positive to encompass, surround, and smother the bad? Why do we constantly remind ourselves of and beat ourselves up with the negative? Instead, we should allow the positive to lift us up! Embrace it! Nurture and grow that which is positive within us, and the negative will have no place to survive!

You see, Christ came to crucify the negative, the sin and the accusations that weigh us down. Remember, the person who Christ sets free is free indeed, as Jesus put in the Gospel of John.

The Bible teaches these lessons in other places. In case you didn't know, the Bible is writings of survival and offers survival skills to live in this broken world.

The Bible has some amazing lessons on how we — you and I — can receive from the heart.

Philippians 4:6-7 NIV – Do not be anxious about anything, but in everything, by prayer and petition, with thanksgiving, present your requests to God. And the peace of God, which transcends all understanding, will guard your hearts and your minds in Christ Jesus.

So, these are the things I want you to take away from this book.

Ready?

Take time to be grateful. To receive from the heart, one must create some space for, and take time to, notice and appreciate!

When is the last time you entered your church and took the time to thank your leadership team or staff for always keeping the place clean? And when I say clean, I mean cleaning up after you!

When is the last time you expressed love and gratitude for your spouse? To your child? To your dear friends? To your family? To God, in thanks for nature?

Let me remind you of a Psalm. "When I see the heavens, the work of Your hands, the moon and the stars which You arranged, what is man that You should keep him in mind, mortal man that You care for him? Yet You have made him little less than a God. With glory and honor You crown him."

The key word in that phrase is "when."When I see. When I recognize. Do we recognize the great gift that we are to our Heavenly Father? We are a part of Him!

Take time to be grateful! Focus on today. Many people can't receive today, because they are so focused on tomorrow.

All too often from my local parish, I hear, "You're leaving tomorrow? Oh, my goodness! What are we going to do? How are we going to sing like we usually do? How are we going to get people in the church?"

The worries go on and on.

But, you know what I say? "You're going to do it by focusing on the day. You're going to realize that you have weekday Mass at the scheduled times, and you're going to get yourself there, because you're going to focus on the day and do what is called of you for that day. You're not just going to say it, you're going to do it, and you're not just going to do it, you're going to live it!"

You may attend Adult Adoration classes that given day, or you may have duties and responsibilities within your occupation or your family, and you're not going to worry about tomorrow, or even about what happened last night or the day before, because you're going to...

Focus on Today!

Miracles

At Midnight on Holy Thursday in 2012, I took the Ciborium with the Eucharist in procession from the church. Catholics believe that from Good Friday until Easter Sunday, the Lord's Body in the Blessed Sacrament is to lie in repose.

In our small parish, the best place for this is in my office attached to the church. I created a sacred space on an old wooden table surrounded with Icons of the Christ and the Blessed Mother. After bowing to the Presence of the Lord, I put a white candle in a glass container.

The next morning, my secretary called me and said, "Father, you need to come to the church right away. There's something in the office, please hurry."

I drove from my home, which is about twenty minutes away. When I walked into the house where my office is located, I gasped.

The entire frame and walls of the waiting room in my office looked like charcoal. My heart sank as I looked toward where I placed the Lord's Body on the wooden table.

I couldn't believe what I saw.

The palm Ciborium, which held the sacrament, didn't burn. In fact, it looked untouched. As I looked around the table, none of the Icons or statues looked harmed. However, the table looked like someone decided to have a barbeque on it.

Then, I looked at the candle wax on the floor. To my surprise, the wax turned into a gold color.

This can't be what it looks like, I thought.

I called the fire department and they came to investigate. Once there, they just stared at the scene.

I asked them, "What's wrong, guys?"

One fireman shook his head. "We can't figure out why this whole place didn't go up in flames."

"What do you mean?" I asked.

He pointed to the scorch marks on the walls. "The best I can tell is that, somehow, the candle got knocked over. The flames raced up the walls, melted everything in this room except…"

The fireman pointed to the Holy Eucharist, "Those things, whatever you call them. They should have melted too, but didn't. The fire in this room was hot and should have taken everything with it."

He shook his head, grabbed his radio and said, "Chief, you need to get over here, we've got one of those religious things going on."

Our town fire chief came over and confirmed the firefighter's assessment. With the radio call, word started getting out in our small parish and town. People from all over came to take pictures and no one could explain what they witnessed.

So, what do I think happened? Technically, I'm not sure. But, I rely on the opinion of the professionals when they say our little church office should be ashes on the ground. Even more, the Eucharist should have been burnt to a crisp. When I take all those facts into consideration, I've got to conclude that some sort of miracle occurred.

Miracles are an embarrassing subject in our modern world. We don't like to talk about them. Our culture relies on science to explain everything. While I love science, and the church encourages scientific study, there's also a key fact we can never ignore.

Science can't explain everything, nor is it meant to do so.

In our little church office, science exhausted every possibility about our fire. The blaze was hot enough to melt metal as it raced through the room at rapid speed. No one could really say how the fire started, or why the candle wax went from a pure white to a golden yellow.

I've no doubt we saw a small miracle and that God spared our parish. Plus, as close together as other houses are on the block, the fire could have endangered lives.

Along with the fire, I've been a firsthand witness to other miracles. For example, during a drive home to visit my mother in Texas. When I reached Nashville, rain began to fall out of the sky in buckets. Water began to pool on the road as I drove a yellow Toyota FJ Cruiser through the large puddles.

I hit one particular puddle and hydroplaned. The Cruiser spun, hit the median, and flipped three times.

When I came to, I found myself hanging upside down. The rescue workers smashed the passenger side window and pulled me out. They asked me, as I bled from head to toe, "Sir, is there anyone with you?"

Horrified, I cried out, "My dog, Sydney, come here girl."

She poked her head out from the car, woofed, and wiggled out.

Then, a strange thing happened. A woman who I met when I presided over her wedding in Portland sent me a text. It said, "Hey, just saw this accident with a car like yours. My husband said I should send it to you so we could all pray for the people in the car."

I chuckled and texted back, "Then I would be praying for myself!"

She called me later, and we had a good, relieved laugh.

Still, as I stared at my car, I knew I probably shouldn't have survived. God watched over me and my dog.

I know people will say, "Yeah, Father, but what about those people around the world who die in car accidents, get their house burned up, or lose their dogs? Do you think you're special to God?"

I do think I'm special to God, just like everyone else in the world. He created us and loves us. But, no, I'm no different from anyone else. I can't tell you why He allowed our church office to go untouched, or why I survived the crash. I do know that He's utilized both situations to His glory.

We think miracles just happen for one purpose. But when we look at the Bible, the miracles always made some point about God and His grace. For example, when Jesus turned the water into wine, not only did He bless the wedding guests with fantastic wine, but He also announced the beginning of His public ministry. And, when Moses parted the Red Sea, God used it to deliver the people of Israel into the Promised Land.

So in other words, miracles are to be shared, talked about, and used for the Glory of God. People need to hear about miracles because they need to know Our Father works in ordinary and extraordinary ways.

He also wants us to see that if we experience miracles in our lives, it's never for our own amusement. While He loves us, He wants us to see that miracles are meant to drive us to love others.

So if your life was saved from a horrible accident, did you ever consider God did so that you might serve the poor in your community? Or maybe He's called you to be a better father, mother, or friend?

Who knows? I can't speak for you, only for myself. I know I share my "miracle" stories to show how God is in hopes it will help someone through a rough time. Plus, miracles don't have to be as dramatic as emerging from a flipped car.

They can just be from the beauty of drawing breath in the morning and being alive with the people who love you.

Change Your Lives!

In high school, I grew up with a group of friends who I loved. We tended to cause a lot of trouble in town and in the parish. Nothing terrible, but we loved to play pranks, be late, and cause problems for everyone around us through thoughtless actions.

For example, when time for Mass on Sunday evening rolled around, we would hang out until the last possible second. Right as the bells chimed, we would run inside so we wouldn't be late.

Of course, my mother already sat in her "registered, trademarked pew" at 5 p.m. sharp.

One day, my buddies and I were hanging around outside the church before weekend Mass. Father Hallahan, the retired, crotchety old priest, who probably grew up with Moses in Egypt, walked by our group as we messed around in our usual spot. We discussed our next prank and what trouble we might cause. (Wish I could remember what we were planning.)

Father Hallahan passed us, and without missing a beat, turned and said to each of us:

"Sichko, Murphy, Ori, and Didyk: change your lives!"

He just kept walking and entered the church. We all stared at each other, a bit gobsmacked and perplexed. I could tell by looking at all of my friends that Father's words struck home. They struck a chord in us that we couldn't explain. If I remember right, our behavior changed and we turned into choir boys.

Okay, so the last part is a bit of an exaggeration, but the point hit home.

We all need the prodding and the encouragement to change our lives! Each of us — whether in work, personality, acceptance, family issues, or personal issues — needs work. We need to take a good look and see what Christ must change in us to make us more like Him.

Change is inevitable. Stability is the illusion. However, growth is optional.

We recognize that we must make choices that govern our lives. Christ and the Holy Spirit help us see the change that must happen in our lives by busting through the barriers in our hearts. As they do, we must look inside, even if it's not very pleasant.

We must see, however, these are times when we grow, mature and become more united with Christ. That is the goal of our lives, really. We can't fight the change if we are to seek Our Lord's face.

I remember speaking once in the Bronx. While presiding at Mass, I invited those at intercessory time to verbalize their prayer, so others in attendance (the community of believers) could share in their prayers, needs, and concerns.

A woman spoke up and, in her prayer, said, "Let us pray first for those who need the words that Father Jim spoke in his homily the most."

Everyone agreed and I started to close the time in prayer when she said, "And let us continue to pray for those who think they need the words that Father Jim spoke the least."

Until we are in the loving arms of our Heavenly Father, each of us should use every moment of our lives to change for the better, and to move forward in recognizing that change. When embraced in a proper way, change can actually bring growth, freedom and inner calm, despite how difficult the thought or process may be to our inner selves.

Remember: change your lives as you move toward being a better person — a Child of God.

Priesthood

Now, I've come to the end of my tale, at least for now. I've got a ton of stories that aren't in this book that I hope to share with you some day. Trust me, I didn't share even a tenth of the stories I could tell. Instead, I chose the ones that fit my little book of Midrash. Someday, you'll get more.

Now, the question I hear most is the one I want to end with: do I love being a priest?

I love being a priest, every moment, even the difficult times. There is no question in my mind that this is what God made me to do. How do I know? Easy. In the dark times, I still love working through the trials, tribulations, and challenges. I love serving the people God gave me to lead.

If I can leave with you a final thought, it would be this: life is too short to just live it half-awake. Even worse, sometimes we see life as a burden, a drudge, or an endless array of misery. Don't get me wrong, life is tough. It can cripple you and leave you full of grief. Yet, at its core, life comes from the Father above who holds everything in His hands.

Acknowledgements

I used to think book writing and publishing could be done alone. How wrong I was! It took a team of supporters, workers and people with drive to get this done. First, I want to thank my parents who taught me how to use my gifts. My brothers and sisters who supported me with love, affection and help. Bill (Sherre), Marifrances (Dan), Sam (Medb), Thereze (Steve); I love you all.

My ecclesiastical family, beginning with Bishop Ronald Gainer, and my brother priests from the Diocese of Lexington. St. Mark Catholic Church in Richmond, Kentucky, who showed patience while their priest wrote a book and does other crazy things.

Bishop Kendrick Williams and Rev. William Brown, thank you for taking a shell shocked young man and turning him into a priest. I love you both of your patience, kindness and trust.

My literary family, beginning with Chas Allen and Jonathan Ryan, who helped me write this book. You helped mold my words into real sentences that could be read by normal people. I'm beyond grateful to both of you.

Italia Gandolfo, my literary agent who landed my book deal and guides me in the dark corners of the book publishing world.

Thomas Ellsworth, CEO of Premier Digital Publishing, for moving heaven and earth to get this book published.

Michael James Canales, who gave me a fantastic book cover using my picture. Now that is saying something.

Finally, to those who were closest to me and didn't know about this book until I sprung it on them fully completed. First, I'd like to thank Jerry and Charlotte Lundergan and their daughters Alissa, Alison, Abby, Ashley, and Amy, for their constant trust in me.

I want to thank Dr. and Mrs. Kent Kessler for believing in this project. Special thanks to Mike and Patty Boyce, Jodie Stockwell and Stephen Bates.

Last, but not least, thanks to my second family, the Invergos: Ben, Regina, Anna, Christine and Emily. I love you all.

To act justly, to love mercy. And to walk humbly with God. Micah 6:8

Contact Information

Father Jim Sichko
Be a part of Father Jim's daily inspirationals and testimonials:
Follow him on Twitter @JimSichko and Facebook:
https://www.facebook.com/jim.sichko
www.frjim.com
Represented by:
Italia Gandolfo, www.ghliterary.com, italia@ghliterary.com

Chas Allen
Discover Chas' projects at www.chasallen.com
Contact Chas personally by email: ChasAllen3@gmail.com
Follow Chas on Twitter @ChasAllen3

Jonathan Ryan
Discover his upcoming novel and articles at
www.authorjonathanryan.com
Follow him on Twitter: @authorjryan and Facebook:
https://www.facebook.com/jryanwriter
Represented by:
Italia Gandolfo, www.ghliterary.com, italia@ghliterary.com

———◦———

Since your life doesn't belong to you, maybe you should use it to serve God and to serve others. Then you can live among friends, and have the real community you crave in the deepest places of your heart. That is what Christ died for, and His gift to you.

Take it. Run with it. Love it. Serve with it, and, at the end, be able to hear those words from the Master: "Well done, good and faithful servant."

Photo Gallery

Fr. Jim on Fox 56

Former First Lady Laura Bush and Fr. Jim

4th-5th Grades of St. Mark Catholic School and Fr. Jim

Harry Connick Jr. and Fr. Jim

Fr. Jim Joining in Prayer with
Pope John Paul II in His Private Chapel

Fr. Jim Concelebrating Morning Mass
in Pope John Paul's Private Chapel

Alex Guzman and Fr. Jim

Bishop Curtis J. Guillory, Ivy Mays Pate and Fr. Jim

Bishop Kendrick Williams and Fr. Jim

Dolly Parton & Fr. Jim

Donny Osmond and Fr. Jim

Former First Lady Laura Bush and Fr. Jim

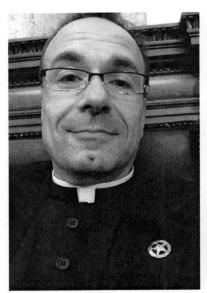

Fr. Jim -
Honorary US Marshall,
Leading Prayer at KY State Senate

Fr. Jim preaching
at St. Peter Catholic
Church in Lexington, KY

Fr. Jim and Sacramento Kings' DeMarcus Cousins

Fr. Jim and Chef John Besh

Fr. Jim and Jason Mraz

Fr. Jim and Pope John Paul II

Fr. Jim and TV-Radio Personality, Lee Cruse

Fr. Jim Harry Connick Jr.

Fr. Jim, President Bill Clinton, Jerry Lundergan

Former KY Secretary of State,
Alison Lundergan Grimes and Fr. Jim

Fr. Jim's Car Accident in Tennessee

Martin Short and Fr. Jim

Rick Springfield and Fr. Jim

Ronald McDonald and Fr. Jim

The Cat in the Hat and Fr. Jim

The Sichko family -
Sam, Bill, Fr. Jim, Thereze, Marifrances, and seated, Marie

Thereze Sichko, Donny Osmond, Marie C. Sichko, Fr. Jim

Thereze Sichko, Marie C. Sichko, Harry Connick, Jr., Fr. Jim

CPSIA information can be obtained at www.ICGtesting.com
Printed in the USA
LVOW06s1306140214

373695LV00002B/2/P